# Playback:

## History Roleplays

## Tim Wood

# Edward Arnold

© Tim Wood 1982

First published 1982
by Edward Arnold (Publishers) Ltd
41 Bedford Square
London WC1B 3DQ

British Library Cataloguing in Publication Data
Wood, Tim
    Playback: history roleplays.
    1. History — Study and teaching
    2. Role playing
    I. Title
    907    D16.2

    ISBN 0-7131-0592-5

*Illustrations* by *Philip Page*

Set by The Castlefield Press of Northampton
Printed in Great Britain by
Butler & Tanner Ltd, Frome and London

# Contents

# Acknowledgements

The Author and Publishers' thanks are due to the following for permission to reproduce copyright photographs:

| | |
|---|---|
| Mary Evans Picture Library: | pp 10, 24b and 26; |
| Bankfield Museum: | pp 11 and 17 |
| Mansell Collection: | pp 22, 33, 34, and 53 |
| Wayland Picture Library: | pp 24t |
| BBC Hulton Picture Library: | pp 25, 44, 47, 57, 58, and 59 |

4

# Introduction

## For the Teacher

### A   Roleplay

Roleplay brings drama into the classroom and allows pupils to experience some events in history at first hand. It is a mixture of scripted play and improvisation. Through roleplay the correct facts and information are transmitted but in an informal and enjoyable manner.

Each roleplay in this book contains historical evidence which is presented by a number of 'witnesses'. The class play the role of 'investigators' seeking the truth by questioning the witnesses closely and thereby extracting the essential information from them.

The class, therefore, come as close as possible to living an historical event. This gives the roleplays an immediacy and relevance while generating excitement and involvement in the class. Pupils are no longer passive receptors of facts but active participants and will find roleplays a painless way to learn.

### B   The Book

This book contains 5 roleplays which appear roughly in order of difficulty. Each one is self-contained and based on a single theme. They are aimed at pupils between the ages of 13 and 17 of all abilities. Each roleplay contains:

a) *An Introduction*   This sets the scene and explains the purpose of the inquiry.

b) *Evidence*   This is usually an original extract and/or a picture or map. It is kept to a minimum but it is always important to the inquiry and will usually provide a useful starting point for the questions.

c) *The roles of the witnesses* The witnesses are named in the introduction to each roleplay. The number in bold type after a witness's name refers to the number of the role, details of which will be found in the back of the book. Witnesses should be called in the order in which they are listed.

IMPORTANT: Only the witnesses and the teacher should refer to the roles during the inquiry. Pupils should be encouraged not to 'snoop'. If they do, a lot of the fun of the roleplay will be lost.

d) *Exercises* There is a selection of graded exercises which teachers may wish to use. They are designed to consolidate the work the pupils have done and to widen the inquiry. The exercises should help pupils develop skills such as forming theories, questioning, examining evidence, detecting bias and coming to realise that there are always different ways of looking at the same event. Much of this work can be done orally or in groups.

## C Operation

The flow chart opposite summarises what you have to do to operate the roleplays.

For teachers who have never used roleplay before there is a section, Further Hints and Advice, on page 92.

**Choose people to play the witnesses**
You can choose these from the class. You can play a role. Senior pupils and other staff can also contribute.

**Prepare class with questions. Introduce topic.**

**The lesson**
Arrange the room as you want. Witnesses can sit in front of the class.

**Go through the introductory material**
Explain the role of the class. Set the scene. Draw pupils' attention to the evidence.

**When all the witnesses have been heard select the appropriate exercise or exercises for individual or group work.**
The roles may be examined for missed details or confirmation of points.

**Brief the witnesses**
1. Witnesses must not lie or make up facts which will affect the inquiry but should try to make their parts lively and interesting by developing a character.
2. They should know their roles well, but not necessarily off by heart. They can refer to the book during questioning.
3. They should reveal rather than conceal evidence, but should make the class work for it.
4. They answer questions rather than reveal information.
5. They can provide 'props' if they wish.

**Make sure outside witnesses know where and when to arrive. Each witness will be questioned for about 10 to 15 minutes.**

**Start the questioning**
1. Call the witnesses one at a time.
2. Get the ball rolling yourself but allow the class to take over as they become more used to it.
3. Start with basic questions — name, job, age, marital status and so on.
4. Questions must be asked one at a time and answers carefully attended. Notes may be taken.
5. Check in the back that evidence is given fully and accurately.
6. Direct or prompt witnesses as needed.
7. Draw the attention of the class to the evidence when necessary.

7

# Advice to Pupils

Many of the characters you will interview in this book will be rather slippery and may not wish to tell you the whole truth. You must question them closely. Here are some points to help you:

a) It will help you to organise the answers under headings such as:

   *Background:* name, job, home, family, etc.

   *History:* How did they get where they are today? What have they been doing in the past few years?

   *Health:* Are they well? If not, why not?

   *Links:* Do they know other witnesses? What do they think of them?

   *Opinion:* What is their view of the situation?

   *Character:* Are they presenting a biased view of the situation? Why?

   You may think of other headings or your teacher may give you more.

b) Look at the written and visual evidence. Ask questions about it. Find out where it fits in.

c) Most important of all **listen** to what is said and **follow up** any little hints that may be dropped.

# 1. The Burning of Mr Swan's Factory

The year is 1812. You are Justices of the Peace (magistrates) in the county of Yorkshire. You have just received news that a factory has been burned down in Wallford. You have gone there yourselves to investigate. You must examine the written and visual evidence and 3 witnesses in order to discover:

a) what exactly happened;
b) who is responsible;
c) why it happened;
d) whether there is likely to be further trouble;
e) what should be done.

## The Witnesses

**Jebediah Swan** — owner of the destroyed factory (24)
**Sarah Head** — a worker (5)
**Matthew Hopkins** — a worker (30)

You know that there have been a number of reports of unrest throughout Nottinghamshire, Yorkshire and Lancashire. Like most landowners you fear that there could be a revolution in England like the one in France in 1789, when many rich people were executed. England has been fighting France on and off ever since (although there is an uneasy peace at the moment) and there may be foreign spies and agents at work stirring up trouble. You must question the witnesses closely in order to discover everything you can in this moment of great danger.

Wallford lies in the heart of Yorkshire and is an important textile-(cloth) producing area.

# Evidence

The 'Spinning Jenny' — a hand-powered textile machine.

We hear in formed that you got Shear in mee sheens and if you Dont Pull them Down in A Forght Nights time wee will pull them Down for you wee will you Damd inferNold Dog. And Bee four Almighty God we will burn down all the Mills that heave Heany Shearing me sheNs in we will cut out A Hall your Damd Hearts as do keep them and we will meock the rest Heat them or else We will seave them the seam.

KiNg Ned Ludd.

*Average weekly earnings of skilled textile workers*

| Year | 1797—1804 | 1804—1811 | 1811— |
|---|---|---|---|
| Wages | 26/8d (£1.34) | 20/— (£1) | 14/7d (73p) |
| Amount of food this bought | 281 lbs | 238 lbs | 131 lbs |

Note: the food is in equal quantities of flour, oatmeal, meat and potatoes

A steam-powered shearing machine.

# Exercises

1. Copy out the following passage, filling in the blanks with words chosen from the list on the next page.

   During the first 20 years of the nineteenth century there were a number of riots. Some of these were caused by the _____ , who were followers of '_____ _____'. They were mostly skilled _____ workers who had been made _____ by steam-powered _____. The riots took place in the counties of _____, _____ and _____. The rioters attacked machines that they thought were putting them out of work, burned down _____ and even killed some _____ _____.

One of the main reasons for the riots was that people were _____ and desperate. The Government sent _____ to stop the riots. The rioters were well-armed and _____. They had many _____ rules and were hard to catch.

| | | |
|---|---|---|
| Nottinghamshire | Lancashire | unemployed |
| factory owners | starving | soldiers |
| secret | textile | machinery |
| Luddites | organised | Yorkshire |
| factories | King Ludd | |

2. Here is a list of things which might have made people become Luddites. Make a table like the one below (yours may be bigger) and fill it in with correct reasons chosen from the list. Add your own explanation for each one.

*Reasons why people became Luddites*

| Reason | Explanation |
|---|---|
| | |
| | |

*Reasons*
a) to get publicity
b) unemployment
c) hating rich people
d) shortage of food
e) the quarrel with France
f) shortage of money
g) encouraged by French spies
h) the war against America
i) to overthrow the Government

3. Complete the word puzzle below.

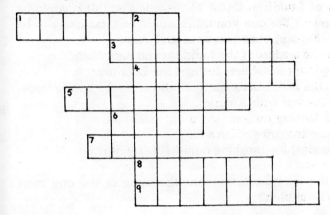

**Down**

2. Rioters who smashed machines (8)

**Across**

1. Another word for cloth (7).
3. Guns used by the rioters (7).
4. The rioters tried to do this to some factories (7).

5. The Government sent these people to stop the riots (8).
6. Swan's factory was 4 across by this (4).
7. The rioters all swore a secret one (4).
8. Large hammers used by the rioters (6).
9. The headquarters of the rioters (8).

4. What evidence was there in the inquiry that each of the following was partly to blame for the riots in Yorkshire, Nottinghamshire and Lancashire:
   a) the Government;
   b) the factory owners;
   c) the workers;
   d) agents, spies and agitators;
   e) local landowners and magistrates?

   Whom do you think was most to blame? Give your reasons.

5. In the inquiry you interviewed 3 witnesses. Comment fully about each of the witnesses on the following points:
   a) Did the witness tell the truth?
   b) Did the witness try to hide anything?
   c) What lies did the witness tell? Why were these told?
   d) Did you find out everything the witness had to tell?

6. Here is a list of possible solutions for the Government to the problem of Luddism. Chose a) the one you think would be fairest and b) the one you think would be most likely to be adopted. Explain your answer in each case.
   a) Find the leaders of the Luddites and hang them.
   b) Bring in more soldiers to fight the Luddites.
   c) Stop the restrictions and limitations on the textile trade.
   d) End the war with America.
   e) Make factory owners stop using machines.
   f) Reduce the price of bread.
   g) Make machine-breaking punishable by death.

   Why is the fairest solution not the same as the one most likely to be chosen?

7. *Discussion:* How accurate and useful was information gathered by spies and agents working for the authorities against the Luddites?

8. *Further research:* Find out about other workers' movements of the time, e.g. Combinations and Chartists. Compare their aims and methods with those of the Luddites.

# 2. Jackson's Mill

The year is 1830. You are a group of important MPs, friends of Lord Shaftesbury. He is investigating conditions in factories in Manchester and he has asked you to find out what you can about Jackson's cotton factory. You do this by looking at the written and visual evidence and examining 5 witnesses.

## The Witnesses

**Mary Taggart** – a worker at Jackson's Mill (27)
**Albert Cook** – a worker at Jackson's Mill (3)
**Henry Beech** – overseer of Jackson's Mill (19)
**Emily Jones** – director of an orphanage in Portsmouth (22)
**Josiah Jackson** – the owner of Jackson's Mill (11)

Lord Shaftesbury is 29 and a notable reformer. He is particularly worried about the conditions of child workers. In 1802 the Health and Morals of Apprentices Act was passed to make working conditions for pauper apprentices (orphans and poor children sold as virtual slave labour to cotton factories) better. The Act established a 12-hour working day for pauper children, and factory inspectors. The 1819 Factory Act stated that no children under the age of 9 should be employed and that children from the ages of 9 to 16 should not work more than 12 hours a day.

Lord Shaftesbury has particularly asked you to find out how successful these Acts have been and what improvements could be made. He intends to bring forward a new Factory Act and needs evidence and suggestions to help him.

## Evidence

# Rules of Jackson's Mill

Any spinner found with his windows open.....
...to be fined  1/-

Any spinner found dirty at his work.......
...to be fined  1/-

Any spinner found washing himself.......
...to be fined  1/-

Any spinner heard whistling.........
...to be fined  1/-

Any spinner being one minute late.......
...to be fined  1/-

Any spinner being sick and cannot find
another spinner to replace him must pay
for steam per day...............6/-

## APPRENTICE ABSCONDED

Run away from Jackson's Mill in Manchester, James DENMAN, a spinner. He is a tall, thin man of 16 years of age.

There is a REWARD for information about his whereabouts.

Advertisement from the *Manchester Mercury*.

A cotton factory.

# Exercises

1. Answer the questions with one word only for each.
   a) What was made in Jackson's Mill?
   b) Where was Jackson's Mill?
   c) What were the factory rules like?
   d) What were the hours of work in the factory like?
   e) What were working conditions in the factory like?
   f) What were the wages in the factory like?
   g) What was a foreman in a factory called?
   h) Were there many other factories like Jackson's Mill?

2. Explain in your own words what a pauper apprentice was.

3. *Is the law being broken in Jackson's Mill?*
   Look at what the laws in 1830 say and in each case choose the sentence which you think best describes what is going on in the Mill.
   a) *The laws say:* Pauper apprentices must not work more than 12 hours a day. In Jackson's Mill:
      i) There are **no** pauper apprentices.
      ii) Pauper apprentices work **more** than 12 hours a day.
      iii) Pauper apprentices work **less** than 12 hours a day.
   b) *The laws say:* Factory inspectors must visit the factory to check on the treatment of pauper apprentices in the Mill.

In Jackson's Mill:
   i) Inspectors **never** visit.
   ii) Inspectors **occasionally** visit.
   iii) Inspectors visit **regularly**.
c) *The laws say:* No children under 9 must be employed. In Jackson's Mill:
   i) **All** the children **are** over 13.
   ii) **All** the children say they are over 13.
   iii) **Some** children **are** under 9.
d) *The laws say:* Children from the ages of 9 to 16 must not work more than 12 hours a day. In Jackson's Mill:
   i) **No** children work **more** than 12 hours a day.
   ii) **Some** children between the ages of 9 and 16 work more than 12 hours a day **sometimes**.
   iii) Children between the ages of 9 and 16 **do work more** than 12 hours a day **quite often**.

Is Jackson breaking the law? Is it his fault?

4. What was it like to work in a cotton factory? Using the evidence of the witnesses to help you, make a table like the one below (yours may be bigger). Fill it in with as many bad points as you can find about working in a cotton factory.

| | Bad points about working in a cotton factory |
|---|---|
| 1. Hours | |
| 2. Wages | |
| 3. Conditions and dangers | |
| 4. Others | |

Why did the factory inspectors allow these bad conditions?

5. a) Draw an advertisement for a job in Jackson's Mill which might be written by the Manager. Emphasise the good points of the job -- factory shop; good wages, pay and conditions; friendly employers, and so on.
b) Now draw another advertisement which shows the job as it really is.

## 6. Complete the word puzzle below.

**Across**

4. James Denman looked this (4).
5. These had to be sent out to work because parents were so poor (8).
8. These were low in the cotton industry (5).
10. Jackson asked for a certificate which showed a worker's ———— (3).
11. Another word for mill (7).
14. The air had to be —— (4) ...
15. or the cotton would —— (4).
16. This part of your body may be trapped in a machine (3).
18. One of these was needed to control the running of factories (10, 3).
20. This was loud in the factory (5).
22. This was harsh in the factory (10).
23. While profits were high, workers were ————— (4).
25. Someone who was 23 across in 1830 (6).
26. Lord Shaftesbury wanted to make factories ————— (5).

**Down**

1. A dirty, run-down house. Mr Jackson owned some (4).
2. Where the pauper apprentices lived before coming to the factory (9).
3. The overseer said the children had to be 'tickled' because they were too ——— (4).
4. Part of a worker's wages was paid in these (6).
6. A result of being poor (6).
7. No machine in a cotton factory had one of these (5).
9. Young men being trained to do a job (11).
12. What came out of a spinning machine (4).
13. The centre of the cotton industry in 1830 (10).
17. A cotton factory foreman (8).
19. After long hours of work the children became this (5).
21. Many factories had their own ————— where the 4 down could be spent (4).
24. The cotton was this before it was spun (3).

7. Factory owners and reformers often saw the factory system in different ways. Make a table like the one below (yours will be bigger). Fill in the table from the list of arguments below. You should finish with 5 arguments in each column.

| Factory owners' arguments | Reformers' arguments |
| --- | --- |
|  |  |

*List of arguments*

1. Factory owners give useful employment to the poor and needy. Without the work the poor would starve.

2. An increase in wages would lead to great increases in the price of cloth. People would buy less, so workers would lose their jobs.

3. Workers are exhausted working the present hours. Shorter hours would mean fresher workers and so more would be produced.

4. If parents were paid more they would not have to send their children out to work.

5. Workers must work long hours to produce the vast amount of cloth needed in England and for export abroad.

6. Guards would cut down the delays and the damage caused by people being dragged into machines. The cost of the guards would soon be paid for by increased cloth production.

7. If people were paid a fair wage there would not be any poor and needy in Britain.

8. Guards on machinery would be expensive. Machines would have to be stopped to be cleaned. This would cause delays and force up the price of cotton.

9. Parents should be allowed to send their children out to work if they want.

10. If workers were paid more they would be better fed and healthier. They could then work harder and so produce more.

For every factory owner's argument there is a reformer's argument, which answers it. Find the pairs of arguments.

8.  Can you find any evidence to suggest that it was not just Jackson who was breaking the law but the workers were also acting illegally?

9.  Write a report for Lord Shaftesbury about the inquiry, covering the following points:
    a)  conditions in cotton factories;
    b)  whether the law is being broken;
    c)  who is to blame;
    d)  what should be done.

10. *1833 Factory Act*

> 1.  No child under 9 to work in a cotton factory.
> 2.  Children between the ages of 9 and 13 not to work more than 9 hours per day and 48 hours per week. They must receive 2 hours schooling per day.
> 3.  Children between the ages of 13 and 18 not to work more than 12 hours per day and 69 hours per week.
> 4.  Four factory inspectors appointed by the Government to enforce the law over the country.

a)  This was the Act that was passed in 1833. What criticisms could you make of it?
b)  What additions would you like to make to it?
c)  Why was it important that the factory inspectors were 'appointed by the Government' and not, as they had been in 1802, by 'local Justices of the Peace'?

A cotton factory.

11. *Discussion*: The state of the Yorkshire textile factories was
described by Richard Oastler, a Yorkshire bailiff, as
'Yorkshire slavery'. Do you agree with him?

Why was factory legislation so slow to develop? What
pressures forced the Government to pass Factory Acts?

Were conditions bad in all textile factories at this time?
Were factory conditions worse than the conditions of
workers under the domestic system?

12. *Further Research*:
   a)   Find out about Robert Owen, Richard Arkwright, Lord
   Shaftesbury and the Ten Hours Movement. What importance
   did each have in the promotion of factory reform?
   b)   Further Factory Acts were passed in 1844, 1847, 1850
   and 1867. Find out what these Acts did. What were their
   strengths and weaknesses?

# 3.  Hertston Prison

It is 1780 in the town of Hertston. The magistrate, Henry Allday, has just died and a new magistrate, Robert Henton, has been appointed. Part of his duty is to inspect the local prison.

You are friends of his, and important people in the town. He has asked you to help him investigate the prison thoroughly. You do this by looking at the evidence and examining 5 witnesses.

## The Witnesses

A prisoner (21)
A prisoner (29)
The jailer (31)
The chaplain (2)
The surgeon (14)

You all know about the book, *State of the Prisons*, recently written by the High Sheriff of Bedfordshire, John Howard. Howard visited over 500 prisons in England and Wales and reported dreadful conditions.

As you well know, crime is greatly on the increase. There are at present over 200 crimes which are punishable by death.

During your questioning you should try to establish what each of the witnesses does; find out how reliable they may be as witnesses; extract as much information as possible about conditions in Hertston Prison; and discover if any of the witnesses can suggest improvements to the situation.

# Evidence

Prisoners in the workshop.

The crank.

| POPULATION OF HERTSTON PRISON AT THE TIME OF THE ENQUIRY : | |
| --- | --- |
| MALE FELONS | : 74 |
| FEMALE FELONS | : 38 |
| DEBTORS | : 67 |
| CHILDREN | : 27 |
| TOTAL | : 206 |

| FEE FOR ENTERING THE PRISON | 2/- |
| --- | --- |
| FEE FOR DISCHARGE | 4/2ᵈ |

HAD THEY BEEN INDUSTRIOUS
WHEN FREE
THEY NEED NOT HAVE
DRUDGED HERE LIKE
SLAVES

The treadwheel (invented in 1818).

The 'Separate System' in action -- prisoners exercise (1862).

# Exercises

1.  Match up each of the prison people with their correct job description. Write them in your books.

| Prison people | Job descriptions |
| --- | --- |
| a) the chaplain | someone in prison for owing money |
| b) the jailer | in charge of the prison workshop |
| c) a felon | ran the whole prison |
| d) a debtor | in prison for a crime like robbery |
| e) the surgeon | in charge of the health of the prisoners |
| f) the manufacturer | in charge of religious matters in prison |
| g) a turnkey | the person supposed to inspect prisons |
| h) the magistrate | in charge of the prisoners in their rooms |

2.  a) Draw diagrams of the **treadwheel** and the **crank** which show clearly how they work. You may label the pictures.
    b) Explain in *full sentences* why they were used in prisons.

26

3. Make a table like the one below.

*Things that were wrong with prisons in 1780*

| List 1 | Top Ten |
|---|---|
| 1. overcrowding<br>2. bad food<br>3. etc. | 1. cruelty<br>2. etc. |

Your table will be bigger than the one shown. Into 'List 1' you will write *all* the things you think were wrong with prisons in 1780. Into 'Top Ten' you will write the ten things you think were the worst, putting them in order, with the worst first. When you have done this, explain why you have chosen your top three things and why you have made them the worst.

4. The money that jailers were allowed to charge the prisoners was called 'fees'.
   a) Make a list of fees the jailer was allowed to charge. You should find about 6 of them.
   b) What are the bad points about charging fees?

5. Make a table like the one shown below into which you write your *own* explanation of each of the different ways the witnesses said that crime could be cured.

| Method | My explanation |
|---|---|
| a) transportation<br>b) 'silent system'<br>c) 'separate system'<br>d) reforming prisoners<br>e) changing society | |

What are the advantages and disadvantages of each method?

6. Complete the word puzzle below.

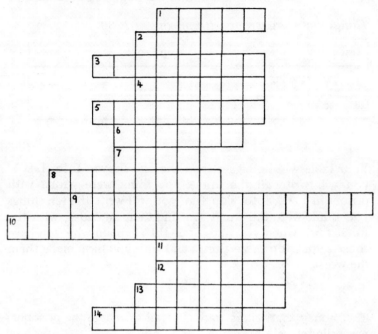

**Down**

1. A way of keeping prisoners apart (8, 6).

**Across**

1. Prisoners slept on this (5).
2. Charges prisoners paid (4).
3. The prison 'vicar' (8).
4. The man in charge of the prison (6).
5. Prisoners needed this to keep healthy (8).
6. Many prisoners wore these (6).
7. Vermin found in prisons (4).
8. They controlled the prisoners (8).
9. This meant prisoners were sent abroad (14).
10. This method stopped the prisoners being a bad influence on each other (6, 6).
11. These often ran through the middle of cells and smelt (6).
12. Jail fever (6).
13. People who owed money (7).
14. New prisoners paid this to buy drinks for everyone (8).

7. Write a report on Hertston Prison for Robert Henton. You should include the following points:
   a) a description of the state of the prison;
   b) which of the prison staff should be commended and which should be blamed;

c) a list of 10 improvements you think should be introduced with an explanation of why you have decided on these.

8. *Who is to blame for the bad state of prisons in 1780?*
Here is a list of people who could all take some blame for the state of prisons in 1780. Explain how each of them is to blame.
a) the visiting magistrates
b) the jailers
c) the turnkeys
d) the prisoners
e) the public
f) the lawmakers
g) society in general
When you have done that, award each of them a percentage to show how much of the blame they should take. The total should not exceed 100%. Give a brief explanation of your decision.

9. Design a prison to replace the old one at Hertston. You can write about it and/or draw a labelled plan of it. You must pay attention to the following points:
a) decent accommodation for prisoners;
b) a hospital (infirmary);
c) separation for various types of prisoners;
d) prison staff near at hand;
e) security — people should not be able to escape;
f) facilities for exercise and worship;
g) work;
h) punishment.

Explain what measures you would take to improve:
a) the staff;
b) the running of the prison;
c) inspection of the prison;
d) reform or punishment of the prisoners.

10. After John Howard had visited over 500 prisons he laid down 4 principles on which he thought the design of prisons should be based. These were:

> 1. The building should be secure, well-ventilated and sanitary.
> 2. Prison staff should be properly paid.
> 3. Prisoners should receive useful training.
> 4. Prisons should be inspected by some outside body.

Do you think these were good principles? What are their strengths and weaknesses? What additions would you like to make to them?

11. *Discussion*:

'Prisons should be made as unpleasant as possible to deter criminals.'

'Prisons should try to reform and help criminals to let them lead a normal life when they have served their sentence.'

Which of these 2 points of view comes nearest to your own?

'The answer to crime lies in the reform of society.'

How far do you agree with this?

12. *Further Research*:

a) Find out what you can about Newgate Prison. Compare it with Hertston Prison.

b) Find out about the work of the following prison reformers: John Howard; Elizabeth Fry; Sir Robert Peel. Explain their contribution to prison reform.

# 4.   Broad Street

It is 1854. The dead body of a tramp, Jack Straw, has been found in Regent Street. There was no sign of violence on Straw's body. Little is known about him except that he was unemployed and lived in a derelict house in Broad Street.

The class take the parts of policemen investigating the death. You must examine the written and visual evidence and 5 witnesses in order to establish:

a)   what caused his death;
b)   the sequence of events that led to his death;
c)   the evidence there is for your conclusion;
d)   what action you think should be taken.

## The Witnesses

Emily Robbins — a friend of Jack Straw (18)
Bert Huggins — owner of the brewery in Broad Street (26)
Mrs Pinch — a director of the workhouse in Poland Street (9)
Professor James Craig — a scientist (33)
Dr John Snow — a doctor (12)

# Evidence

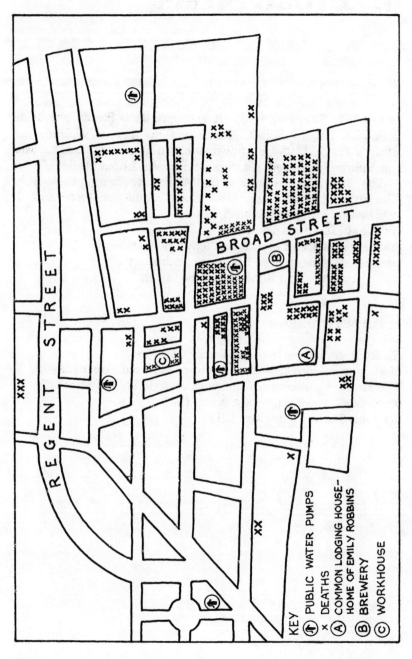

KEY

🕴 PUBLIC WATER PUMPS
X DEATHS
Ⓐ COMMON LODGING HOUSE–
   HOME OF EMILY ROBBINS
Ⓑ BREWERY
Ⓒ WORKHOUSE

REGENT STREET

BROAD STREET

A street in London.

Faraday the great scientist presenting his card to Father Thames.

# Exercises

1.  Choose the correct ending to this sentence:
    The most *likely* cause of the death of Jack Straw was
    a)  murder.
    b)  accident.
    c)  old age.
    d)  disease.
    e)  suicide.

2. Choose the correct ending to this sentence:
   I think this because
   a) lots of people had been murdered in Broad Street.
   b) Jack Straw was very unpopular.
   c) Jack Straw was rich.
   d) Broad Street was not a healthy place in 1854.
   e) Jack Straw was very old.
   f) Jack Straw was feeling very depressed.
   g) there were wounds on Jack Straw's body.

3. Answer these questions about the witnesses.
   a) Who lived in a common lodging house?
   b) Who said Jack Straw had no enemies?
   c) Who said cholera was a punishment from God?
   d) Who thought heavy drinking caused cholera?
   e) Who drank heavily and did not catch cholera?
   f) What did Dr Snow believe had caused the cholera?
   g) What did Professor Craig believe had caused the cholera?

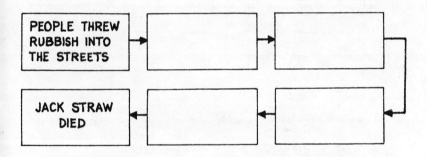

4. Copy out the chart above. Put the 4 sentences below into the right order and then write 1 sentence into each of the 4 empty boxes to show the correct chain of events which led to Jack Straw's death.

   Jack Straw drank the water.
   Cholera germs grew in the dirty water.
   The dirt soaked into the cracked clay water pipes.
   The dirty water came out of the Broad Street pump.

5. Explain what a workhouse was.

6. Complete the word puzzle below.

## Down

1. This killed Jack Straw (5, 6, 4).

## Across

1. Workers here did not catch cholera (7).
2. This thrown into the street caused dirt to get into the water (7).
3. People who were like this went into the workhouse (3).
4. Some people said drinking this *cured* cholera — others said it *caused* cholera (7).
5. There is no doubt cholera was this (9).
6. These pipes could also pollute the water supply (6).
7. Huggins thought Straw was one of these (5).
8. Huggins' beer travelled by this excellent new form of transport (7).
9. This witness said Jack Straw had no enemies (5, 7).
10. When many people die of a disease it is called this (8).
11. One of the effects of cholera was to cause this to rise (11).
12. People took these to avoid catching cholera (11).
13. Emily said Jack Straw had been this for over two years (10).
14. People *used* this as a 12 across against cholera (7).
15. People *said* these as a 12 across against cholera (7).

7. Answer the following questions:
   a) Dr Snow found no cholera germs in the water from the Broad Street pump. Why was this?
   b) Dr Snow still said the Broad Street pump was the cause of the cholera. Give as many reasons as you can which explain why he thought this.
   c) Why was the evidence given by Mrs Pinch and Bert Huggins so important?

8. Study the following statements. Write down only those which you think could be proved from the facts you have read and heard and from common sense. Give your reasons for each one you write down.
   a) All public water pumps in London are a health hazard.
   b) There is no evidence that the Broad Street pump is any more dangerous than any other public water pump.
   c) Only people who drank from the Broad Street pump died of cholera.
   d) People who did not drink from the Broad Street pump stood a much better chance of escaping from cholera than those who did.
   e) Although evidence points to the fact that cholera in Broad Street was caused by water from the Broad Street pump, it may, in fact, have been caused by something quite different.
   f) Cholera could only be caught from the Broad Street pump.
   g) Overcrowded houses cause cholera.

9. Write a report on the Broad Street inquiry, covering the following points:
   a) the most probable explanation of Jack Straw's death;
   b) how and why he died;
   c) the evidence there is for your conclusion.

10. Here are 5 possible courses of action which the Public Health Officer could take. Write down the advantages and disadvantages of each.
   a) Accept the fact that people are bound to die from cholera and so do nothing about the pump.
   b) Advise people not to use the Broad Street pump but to go to one of the other pumps further away.

c) Advise people to boil water from the Broad Street pump before drinking it.

d) Remove the handle of the pump so people cannot use it.

e) Try to find out why the water is polluted and correct the fault.

11. *Discussion*: Why were cities and towns so slow to take measures to safeguard public health?

12. *Further Research*

a) The 1866 Sanitary Act made local authorities appoint sanitary inspectors and 'suppress nuisances'. What nuisances were there in towns in Victorian England which were a hazard to health?

b) Discover what you can about the contributions of Edwin Chadwick and Lord Shaftesbury to public health.

c) A Public Health Act was passed in 1848. Why did it not prevent the Broad Street epidemic? Other Public Health Acts were passed in 1866, 1872 and 1875. What were the main terms of these Acts? What were their shortcomings?

# 5. Westford Workhouse

The year is 1842. You are all members of the Board of Guardians which runs a workhouse in the Westford Union. You are meeting to review the situation in the workhouse and to interview 3 married couples for the jobs of Master and Matron of the workhouse.

## Historical background

You all remember well the bad old days before 1842 when the old system of giving Poor Relief to paupers became too expensive. The system used to encourage the poor to be lazy, to live off the Parish Poor Rate and not to look for work. There was much corruption and inefficiency in the way local officials ran the system. A number of different methods of Poor Relief were used throughout the county.

In 1834, the Poor Law Amendment Act was passed which introduced a new and what you consider to be much more efficient Poor Law. The Act said that unemployment and poverty were caused by the idleness and bad habits of the poor. To deal with this the Act set up a central and unified system of Poor Relief. The Act said:

1. Parishes should be grouped together into Unions. Each Union would have its own workhouse.
2. Poor Relief would only be given to paupers who went into a workhouse. There would be no outdoor relief for paupers who were well enough to work.
3. Paupers should be encouraged to find work, so conditions in the workhouse were to be made as unattractive and uncomfortable as possible.
4. Boards of Guardians were to be formed. These were elected ratepayers who would be responsible for the operation of the Poor Law in their Union.

You are all important members of the county. You all firmly believe that people are poor because of their own faults, laziness and bad management. You think that paupers should be encouraged to work and should not think of the workhouse as a rest home or a comfortable hotel. The workhouse is there to stop them starving. You want to see the paupers in your care learning better habits, better morals and improving themselves. You want the paupers to develop self-discipline so smoking and drinking are not allowed. Many of you think that more religion could provide the answer for them.

Although the workhouse is bleak and strict, you are proud of it. You are sure that the paupers are being cured of their bad ways there. You are also sure that the workhouse is efficiently and fairly run within the new law. You do not want any of the cruelty that is sometimes reported in other Unions.

Your work at this meeting of the Board of Guardians is in 4 stages. (Teachers may distribute roles 1, 4, 8, 10, 13, 17, 20, 23, 25, 28, 32 and 36 throughout the class at the start of stages 1, 2 or 3 as desired. Teachers see page 95 for further hints on this roleplay.)

### Stage 1   Checking that all is as it should be in the workhouse

You wish to check that the Poor Law is being correctly and fairly run in Westford Union. You are going to make a thorough and careful investigation of the workhouse. Your teacher will divide you into groups and give each group one set of exercises (from exercises 1—5) to complete.

Each group will then prepare a short report on the aspect of the workhouse it has studied.

### Stage 2   Discussion of the investigation

When the exercises have been completed each group will read out its report to the Board. The Board will discuss the Poor Law and the operation of the workhouse. You should decide:
a)   what your own attitude to the poor is;
b)   what conditions in the workhouse are really like;
c)   what the aims of the Board of Guardians are and whether these aims are being carried out;
d)   what kind of Master and Matron are wanted to run the workhouse.

The Board can then discuss the job and draw up a list of questions and points they wish covered in the interviews.

## Stage 3    Interviewing the candidates

The candidates for the job of Master and Matron are then interviewed.

# The candidates (witnesses)

Mr Frederick Rushbrook (15) and Mrs Jane Rushbrook (16)
Mr Joseph Bridge (6) and Mrs Emily Bridge (7)
Mr Samuel Wallis (34) and Mrs Sarah Wallis (35)

This is the advertisement that was posted:

# WANTED

A MASTER AND MATRON FOR THE WORKHOUSE IN WESTFORD. THEY MUST BE IN THE MIDDLE AGE OF LIFE, WITHOUT CHILDREN AND OF GOOD CHARACTER.

You must try to find out as much as possible about the following:
1. Firstly, the character and background of the candidates. What experience have they? Are they of good character? Are they suitable people to run a workhouse? You should be warned that candidates may be evasive on certain points. You must question them closely. Remember, the job is not very well-paid. Why do they want it?

2. Secondly, find out how the candidates see the job. How will they run the workhouse? Will they change it for the worse? How will they treat the paupers?

When all the candidates have been interviewed the Board can discuss them. A vote can be taken. The Board *must* appoint one of the couples.

### Stage 4  Follow-up

Your teacher may wish to reveal certain information about the candidates which you may not have discovered.

You then complete some or all of the follow-up exercises (6—12) as directed by your teacher. You may wish to complete those sections of exercises 1—5, which you have not already done.

# Exercises

## 1. The Paupers

*Figures to show the number of inmates in the workhouse in 1842*

| MEN (aged over 13) | Total = 61 | of these | 12 are married<br>36 unmarried<br>13 widowed<br>8 over 65 years of age<br>2 deaf and dumb<br>2 idiots<br>47 were agricultural labourers |
|---|---|---|---|
| WOMEN (aged over 16) | Total = 30 | of these | 9 married<br>13 unmarried<br>8 widowed<br>5 over 65 years of age |
| BOYS | Total = 51 | | |
| GIRLS | Total = 56 | | |

Paupers were divided into 3 groups:
1. Able-bodied — these were adults (under 65 years of age) who were well enough to work.
2. The aged and infirm — these were people who were old (over 65) or were too ill to work.
3. Children — boys under 13 and girls under 16.

Look carefully at the table and answer these questions:
1. What is the total number of paupers in the workhouse?
2. What is the total number of able-bodied paupers (ie. sane, healthy and under 65 years of age)?
3. What is the total number of aged or infirm paupers?
4. What is the total number of child paupers?
5. Why are there so many agricultural labourers in the workhouse?
6. What is the maximum number of complete families there can be in the workhouse at the moment?
7. Give 2 reasons to explain why there are so many children in the workhouse.
8. What evidence is there that the workhouse is helping people?
9. What were the main reasons for people being in the work-house?

## 2.  The Workhouse

This is a picture of the workhouse.

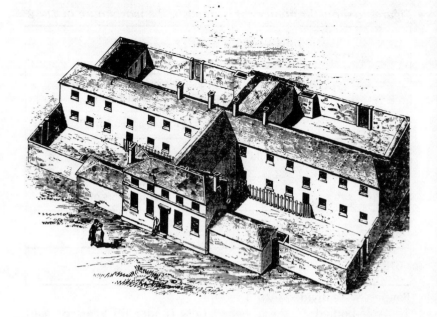

Look carefully at the picture above and the plan opposite to help you answer these questions:
1.  What evidence can you find that men, women, boys and girls did not mix freely in the workhouse?
2.  Why were the Master's rooms (where the Master and Matron lived) placed in the middle of the workhouse?
3.  Look at your answers for 1 and 2. What do you think would happen to a family which came to the workhouse?
4.  What reasons would the Board of Guardians give for doing this?
5.  What evidence can you find that the workhouse helped sick people?
6.  What evidence is there that children received an education in the workhouse?
7.  Look at the following rooms: 2, 3 and kitchen. What were some of the jobs women might do in the workhouse?
8.  What do you think the social life of the paupers was like?
9.  Is there any evidence that paupers were ill-treated?

This is a plan of the workhouse.

Ground level

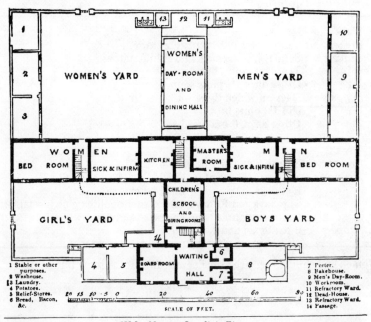

1 Stable or other purposes.
2 Washhouse.
[3 Laundry.
4 Potatoes.
5 Relief-Stores.
6 Bread, Bacon, &c.

7 Porter.
8 Bakehouse.
9 Men's Day-Room.
10 Workroom.
11 Refractory Ward.
12 Dead-House.
13 Refractory Ward.
14 Passage.

SCALE OF FEET.

[K.] No. 2. One Pair Plan.

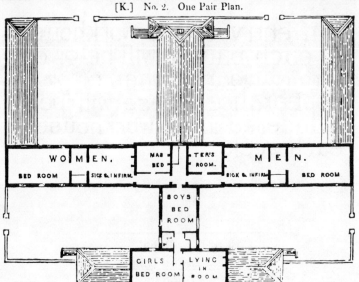

First floor

45

## 3. Food

*Workhouse Dietaries (men)*

---

**Week 1**
*Breakfasts*: 6 ozs bread and 1½ ozs cheese.
*Dinners*   : Sundays, 5 ozs meat and ½ lb potatoes.
               Tuesdays and Thursdays ditto.
               Other days 1½ pints soup.
*Suppers*   : Days on which there was meat for dinner, 6 ozs bread
               and 1½ pints broth.
               Other days, 6 ozs bread and 2 ozs cheese.

**Week 2**
*Breakfasts*: 6 ozs bread and 1 oz cheese.
*Dinners*   : Sundays, 16 ozs of meat pudding plus vegetables.
               Mondays, 7 ozs bread and 1 oz cheese.
               Tuesdays and Fridays, 16 ozs suet pudding plus vegetables.
               Other days, bread and cheese as Mondays.
*Suppers*   : 6 ozs bread and 1 oz cheese.

---

Women and children received smaller amounts of the same things.

---

On entry to the workhouse each pauper will be given strong clean clothes of plain appearance. These will be laundered in the workhouse each week.

---

Cost of Poor Relief
in the Westford Union.
1830 — £14,567
1842 — £8,329

---

A workhouse yard in the 1840s. Notice that the women have a separate yard from the men and are all wearing the same workhouse dress.

Look at the evidence above and on the opposite page to help you answer the questions:
1. Make a table like the one shown on the next page to show the workhouse meals through the week. Your table will be much bigger and remember there are 2 menus.

| DAY | MENU | BREAKFAST | DINNER | SUPPER |
|---|---|---|---|---|
| MONDAY | WEEK 1 | | | |
| | WEEK 2 | | | |
| TUESDAY | WEEK 1 | | | |
| | WEEK 2 | | | |
| ETC. | | | | |

2. Look carefully at the food the paupers ate. Which of the sentences below describe the food best? (There may be more than one.)

   a) The workhouse provided meals that could be found in the best hotels.

   b) The food was interesting and varied.

   c) The food was boring.

   d) The food was better than the paupers would eat outside the workhouse.

   e) Paupers were deliberately starved to death by workhouses.

   f) The menus were carefully designed to provide enough food for the paupers.

   g) The menus were designed to save money.

   h) The meals were cheap and nutritious (enough to keep them healthy).

3. Explain why there was not much meat for the paupers.

4. Describe the paupers' clothes. Give 2 reasons why they were given these clothes.

5. Why do you think most paupers hated the clothes they were given when they came to the workhouse?

6. What was the purpose of keeping the meals and clothes simple?

7. Why would the Board of Guardians have been pleased with the figures for Poor Relief given above?

8. Can you find any evidence of cruelty to the paupers?

## 4. Rules

These are the rules of the workhouse

Any pauper who does not obey the rules...
Or who does not keep silent when told to...
Or who swears or uses bad language...
Or threatens to hit anyone...
Or refuses to work when told to...
Or plays cards or other gambling games...
Will be called DISORDERLY.

Any pauper who breaks these rules again within a week...
Or who insults or is rude to the Master, Matron or any other officer of the workhouse..
Or who gets drunk...
Or who deliberately disturbs others during prayers or worship...
Will be called REFRACTORY.

## PUNISHMENTS FOR DISORDERLY PAUPERS
The Master of the workhouse can give them bread and water for 2 days and not allow them butter, cheese, tea, sugar or soup.

## PUNISHMENTS FOR REFRACTORY PAUPERS
The Board of Guardians can order them to be put in a room by themselves for 24 hours on a diet of bread and water.

# EXTRACT FROM THE PUNISHMENT BOOK

| Name | Offence | Date | Punishment |
|------|---------|------|------------|
| Ann Ward | Stealing 6 oz bacon from the store. | 1/10/1840 | 8 hours in lock-up. Bread and water. |
| John Pike | Smoking in bed. | 14/12/1840 | Tea and sugar stopped. |
| Maria Cooke | Refusing to work | 3/2/1841 | 4 hours in lock-up. |
| George Leech | Drunk | 8/2/1841 | Bread and water for 2 days. |
| Henry Frost | Refusing to work | 18/3/1841 | Bread and water for 2 days. |

## TOTAL PUNISHMENTS FOR 1840 ~ 16
## TOTAL PUNISHMENTS FOR 1841 ~ 29

Look at the evidence above and on the previous page carefully and answer the questions below:

1. What punishments could be given to paupers who did not obey the rules?
2. Would you describe these punishments as cruel?
3. Why was John Pike punished? Do you think he deserved punishment? Explain your answer.
4. Not all the rules are included in the extracts but in each case above decide if the paupers were disorderly or refractory.
5. Do you think there were a large number of punishments in the years 1840 and 1841? (There were roughly 200 inmates.)

6. How would you describe the discipline in the workhouse? Choose some suitable words from this list: cruel; harsh; strict, unfair; reasonable; easy-going; pleasant; firm.
7. Give evidence from the facts above to show each of the following points:

   a) that paupers were being cured of bad and expensive habits;

   b) that paupers were given moral and religious education to improve them;

   c) that good habits of hard working were being drilled into them;

   d) that they were being taught self-discipline.
8. Explain what the main aims of the rules were.

## 5. Routine

*Girls* do household duties — washing floors, making beds, washing, ironing, knitting and sewing. They learn the duties of a maid, a dairy maid, a lady's maid, a nurse and how to run a family. They are taught to cook. They are taught the most economical way to run a household. They receive many warnings of the dangers of overspending and careless accounting.

*Boys* receive education and religious and moral training. They learn how to make and repair their clothes and shoes. They do gymnastic exercises and gardening. They are taught reading, writing and arithmetic. They receive other instruction suitable for their station in life. They are taught how to make tin ware and how to blacksmith. They are trained in the habits of usefulness, industry and virtue.

*Men* pick oakum (untwist old ropes), crush bones and break rocks which are used for road repairing and building.

*Women* do household work.

---

*Timetable*

| | |
|---|---|
| 6.00 a.m. Rise, wash, dress, rollcall | 2.00 p.m. Work for adults; school for children |
| 6.30 a.m. Prayers; Breakfast (eaten in silence) | 4.00 p.m. Prayers, religious instruction |
| 7.15 a.m. Exercise in the yards | 5.00 p.m. Hymn singing; giving thanks to God |
| 8.00 a.m. Work | |
| 11.00 a.m. Prayers, Bible reading, hymns | 6.00 p.m. Supper (eaten in silence) |
| 12.00 noon Lunch (eaten in silence) | 6.30 p.m. Religious service |
| 12.30 p.m. Exercise in yards | 9.00 p.m. Bed |

A workhouse dormitory. Notice the mottoes on the walls.

53

# RULES

1. Any pauper can leave the workhouse if the Master is given 4 hours notice.
2. A man with a family can only leave if he takes his family with him, except if he is looking for work.
3. No visitors allowed without permission from the Master. Visitors must be seen in the presence of the Master or Matron.
4. Mothers may talk to their children if they are below the age of 7. Married couples may only visit each other if there is some special reason, such as illness, with permission from the Master.

Look at the evidence above and on the previous pages to help you answer the questions below:

1. What evidence is there that boy paupers received useful training which could help them find work?
2. What was the point of the training the girl paupers received?
3. What differences are there in the treatment of adults and children? Explain why there are these differences.
4. What kind of things are written on the workhouse walls? Why are they there? What effect are they supposed to have on the paupers?
5. What kind of things would children have been taught in moral education? Why were they taught these things?
6. Why were meals eaten in silence?
7. Why were prayers and religious services such an important part of workhouse life?
8. How would you describe life for the paupers in the workhouse? Choose suitable words from this list: fun; hard; horrible; difficult; rewarding; strict; uncomfortable; amusing; dull; lively; monotonous; cruel.
9. Why was life in the workhouse made like this?
10. Why did paupers stay in the workhouse when they could leave quite easily?

# Follow-up Exercises

6. Complete the word puzzle below (the clues are on the next page).

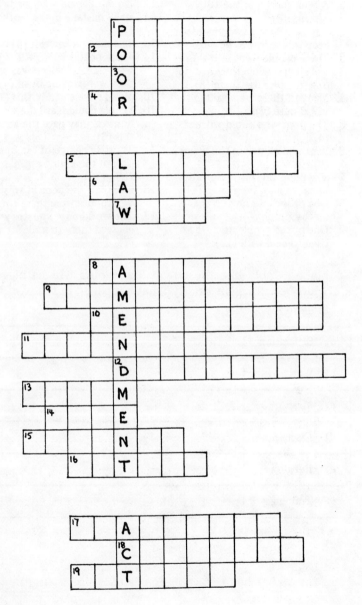

## Down
1. The new Poor Law of 1842.

## Across
1. A poor person in the 19th century (6).
2. The new Poor Law aimed to keep this as low as possible (4).
3. These people went into the workhouse when they had no one to look after them (3).
4. Many of these were said in the workhouse (7).
5. The poor who could work (4, 6).
6. Person in charge of the women (6).
7. The poor did this in the workhouse to earn their keep (4).
8. One of the areas which made up the Union (6).
9. One of the problems 1 Down tried to deal with (12).
10. A poor person who behaved very badly in the workhouse (10).
11. The young received this to help them find work (8).
12. A poor person who made a small mistake in the workhouse (10).
13. The men picked this (5).
14. Many people thought the poor were _____ which was why they were unemployed (4).
15. Meals were eaten in this (7).
16. People could leave the workhouse if they gave the Master this (6).
17. Those in charge of the operation of the Poor Law in a Union (9).
18. Over half the poor in Westford Workhouse were these (8).
19. The workhouse inmates were allowed there to look for work (7).

7. Make a table like the one below (yours will be bigger) in which you explain briefly what happened in the workhouse about each of the following:

| a) Separation | |
| --- | --- |
| b) Work | |
| c) Meals | |
| d) Discipline | |
| e) Religion | |
| f) Training | |

8. Study this picture of a workhouse and answer the questions below:
   a) Where are these men?
   b) What are they doing?
   c) Who is the man labelled A? What is he doing?
   d) Explain exactly what each of the men labelled B, C and D are doing.
   e) What is the artist trying to tell us about workhouses?
   f) Explain why this may not be a completely truthful picture.
   g) Why might the artist have painted a false picture?

9. Write a report about the Westford Workhouse. Try to cover the following points:
   a) conditions in the workhouse (the building, work, rules, discipline, moral education, inmates etc);
   b) what the aims of the 1834 Poor Law were;
   c) which candidates were selected and why;
   d) what problems may occur in the workhouse from now on.

Photo A

10. a) Describe briefly the methods of Poor Relief in England before 1834.

b) What views are being expressed about the methods of the Poor Relief before 1834 in photo A? What other criticisms were also made of the methods?

Photo B

c) What views are being expressed in photo B about the system of Poor Relief set up in 1834?

d) Describe briefly the changes made in 1834 and show how far the views expressed in photo B were justified in fact.

e) Do you think the artist supports either system? Explain your answer.

11. *Discussion:*

Why did the Victorians believe that poverty was the fault of the poor?

Why were the public so slow in demanding reform of the workhouse system?

12. *Further research*

Find out all you can about the following:

a) Samuel Smiles and 'self-help'

b) Edwin Chadwick and the Poor Law

c) The Royal Commission 1905—9 and the causes of pauperism

d) The Reforms of the Liberal Government 1905—15

e) The ideas of *laissez faire*

# Roles

1.   You are an important member of the local church. You are very anxious that there should be no reduction in the time the paupers spend in religious instruction and going to services. You will want to know all about the moral habits of the candidates. What sort of girls were in Mrs Rushbrook's lodging house? Why is her face so red?

2.   You are the vicar of the nearby parish of Hertsford. You are a very strict churchman who hates any kind of ungodly behaviour. Your sermons on the evils of drunkenness and debauchery are famous for miles around. Weaker members of the congregation have been known to faint in the middle of them.

You have acted as chaplain of Hertston Prison for 2 years. You visit the prison twice a week at least, often more. You take your job very seriously and keep careful records. You are extremely critical of conditions there.

*Your importance to the inquiry — try to make the following points:*

a)   The staff of the prison are ungodly, untrained and incompetent. The jailer rarely bothers to go into the prison. The turnkeys are all brutes (sons of Satan) who will stop at nothing to hurt and humiliate the prisoners.

b)   Worse than this, there are no provisions at all for church services. There is no chapel. There is the atmosphere 'of Hell' and the works of the Devil are to be seen at every hand. The staff never go to church and are, in most respects, as bad as the prisoners they are meant to guard.

c)   Drink is freely available in the prison taproom. Any inmate with the money is allowed to get drunk. This means that there are often scenes of drunkenness and debauchery too horrible to recount (not that this will stop you). There are often fights among the prisoners. Several have been killed over the last few years. The taproom is the work of the Devil and only benefits the jailer and the staff who get a share of the profits.

d) It is a well-known and proven fact that criminal tendencies are a disease, like smallpox or measles, and are highly contagious. Despite this the prisoners are all mixed together with no thought given to the results.

It is hardly surprising that with men mixing freely with women there are many problems. Several babies have been born inside the prison, brought about partly by the rule that pregnant women cannot be hanged. How can these little children have any hope being brought up in this Hellish atmosphere?

e) Children who have committed any crime, however trivial, are also sent to prison where they mix with hardened criminals and no doubt are led into evil by them.

f) Worse still, the innocent are mixed with the guilty. People waiting for trial, who may later be found innocent, are subjected to this horror and no doubt many catch the criminal disease.

g) The system of hard labour where prisoners saw stone and break rocks is too hard. Many are weak from lack of food and the women do the same work as the men.

*Your solutions:*

At present it is obvious that prison does nothing to *reform* criminals. In fact just the opposite is true because prisons encourage and increase evil tendencies. Facts show that once a person has been sent to jail they will almost certainly return. The answer is to reform criminals. They must be brought to more moral ways by the teachings of the Bible.

a) Prisoners must be separated from each other. The so-called 'Separate System' should be introduced. A new prison must be built where each prisoner has his or her own cell. This would stop the disease of criminality from spreading and also cut down the spread of other diseases like typhus.

The hardest criminal can be brought to his senses by a period of solitary confinement. You have countless examples of evildoers who have turned to God, weeping in your arms after isolation.

b) There should be separate prisons for men and women. There should be different arrangements made for children.

c) Prisoners should be visited regularly by Churchmen. They would soon be convinced by loneliness and praying that their only hope lies in God. There should be plenty of church services in a special chapel.

d) The prison staff must be trained properly. Only people of good character should be employed. There should be a proper rule book and jailers should be paid a good salary.

e) Drink should not be available to prisoners.

f) Hard labour should stop except for very serious crimes.

g) Proper training and education should be given to prisoners so that they can find a decent job when they leave and not fall back into the temptations of crime.

3. You are a young lad of 12 who works at Jackson's Mill. Your mother died of smallpox when you were a baby. Your father, who works in a local iron foundry, brought you up. Your younger brother, aged 11, also works in the mill. You walk with a heavy limp because for three years your job was leaning over the top of a working machine in an awkward position to work a lever — as a result, your spine is crooked and one leg is shorter than the other. A number of other children in the factory have similar, or worse, deformities. The only work you can do now is working as a sweeper in the cotton store, where the air is thick with dust and cotton threads. You have recently started to cough blood.

You are very worried about your small brother who has recently been given a job machine-cleaning. This involves crawling in and out of the working machines. As he is so tired because of the long hours (14 hours a day), you fear that, like many other children, he may fall asleep and be dragged into a machine.

*Your importance to the inquiry — try to make the following points:*

a) The hours are very long. This makes the workers tired and slow. It is especially bad for those children who have to walk a long distance to work.

b) You have heard plenty of horror stories about exhausted children falling into machines or crying with fatigue.

c) Many of the children at Jackson's Mill are under the age of 12 — some as young as 6. You know they are all supposed to produce certificates to say they are 13 and physically fit, but Mr Beech often does not bother to ask for them and anyway they are easy to obtain — a fit lad can make a tour of local doctors getting a certificate from each one and then selling them to children wanting employment.

d) The wages at the factory are very low — 6d (2½p) a week for children and of this only 3d (1½p) is paid in cash. The rest is in tokens which can be exchanged for food at Mr Jackson's shop. The prices there are double those anywhere else. You have to work because your father does not earn much.

e) You live near the factory in a house owned by Mr Jackson. The rent is high and the property is in a disgusting state. Anyone who gets behind with the rent is thrown out into the streets.

f) Conditions in the factory are very bad. It is very hot and noisy. There are lots of strict rules.

g) Mr Beech is a brute. He flogs children unmercifully with his heavy leather belt for no reason at all. He drinks too much and is always swigging a bottle of rum. When drunk, he is a devil and will become uncontrollably angry. He sometimes tortures workers he does not like — loading them with heavy weights to make their work even harder.

h) Although there are some pauper apprentices, the children are mainly the sons and daughters of workers at the factory.

i) Normal hours of work at the factory: 6a.m. to 8p.m.
Hours of work during brisk time (a period of extra work): 3a.m. to 9p.m.
Normal pay for adults: 3/- per week (15p)
Wages during brisk time: 3/7½ (18p)
Wages for children — maximum : 2/- per week (10p)
                    usual : 6d per week (2½p)
Pauper apprentices earn nothing.

4.   You are an important member of the local church. You feel that the present amount of moral education in the workhouse is too small. You want paupers to spend more time thanking God that they are well cared for. A stronger line should be taken with drunkenness and laziness. Too much money should not be spent on the ungrateful.

5.   You are 25 and married with 4 children. You are completely uneducated and rather overawed by the important people interviewing you. You and your husband used to work in Swan's factory until a year ago. Your husband was a shearer (skilled cutter and finisher of cloth). You worked a hand-operated

spinning machine. Both of you lost your jobs when Mr Swan bought steam-driven machines. These machines can do the jobs of several people so many workers were laid off, yourselves among them. Since then you have had a desperate time. Your husband works when he can, sometimes doing dangerous work in the nearby lead mine. You keep a very small patch of land and do farming work when you can get it. You sometimes walk to farms 20 miles away to find work.

*Your importance to the inquiry —try to make the following points:*

a) There is a great deal of unemployment among textile workers in the area caused by the coming of machines. Also the wages of those who are still working have dropped steadily (see table on page 11). Many people are starving. There have been food riots over a wide area. Many textile workers who used to be well-off now dress in rags.

b) You are worried about your children who are thin and ill. If you cannot get work soon you are sure that one of them will die. You live in a tumbledown cottage which leaks and is cold in winter. You can hardly afford the rent and may be thrown out. You have sold most of your possessions and furniture to buy food. Many other workers are now in this position.

c) You heard a lot of noise near Swan's factory last night and the sound of guns firing. You later heard noises and shouting in the village. You and the family stayed inside with the doors firmly bolted.

d) You are not surprised that the factory has been burned down. Swan is a cruel employer who has reduced wages and thrown people out of work. He cares nothing for the poor.

e) You believe that the fire was probably the work of Luddites. These are followers of 'King Ludd' who smash the machines that are putting people out of work. You have never been to a Luddite meeting. You do not know any Luddites. You would not help the Luddites under any circumstances.

This is all you know. If other questions are asked you become agitated and frightened. Like most of the villagers you know nothing and can say nothing.

*Your solutions:*

You think the Luddites are desperate people. The problem will not be solved until employers are paying fair wages and get rid of their machines. The machines in any case do not do the jobs as well, just quicker.

**6.** (Information in brackets to be kept secret as long as possible.)

Born in 1794. Your father was a clergyman in the Church of England. You received a good education with a private tutor. (You hated him and spent most of your time hiding from him.) In 1812 you became an Army Chaplain. You were in the 89th Foot Regiment. In 1815 you left the Army with a distinguished record. (In fact you were given a dishonourable discharge for gambling debts and duelling.)

In 1816, through your Army connections with Lord Hazleton, who was in your regiment (and your gambling companion), you were fixed up as a country parson in Sussex. From 1815 to 1842 you have been a successful and well-loved vicar (with a number of scandalous affairs and heavy gambling debts). You can provide excellent references from several important Sussex landowners and Churchmen. (They have been trying to get rid of you and have now told you to leave the county or face prison.)

You are respectable and sober in appearance. You should be a strong candidate for the job if you can keep your gambling secret. If the Board wants to know why you are taking a cut in salary and are prepared to move to this humbler job you can talk about the voice of God telling you to give up your comforts and help poor sinners.

You would continue to run the workhouse very much as it is at the moment (although you do not intend to stay there for long — just till the dust has settled). You would increase the religious and moral education of the young paupers and preach many fiery sermons about the sin of poverty.

**7.** (Information in brackets to be kept secret for as long as possible.)

Born in 1810. Your father was a gentleman farmer. Your family was respectable and honest. You fell in love with Joseph and married him in 1830. He was an impressive young man.

You are not in very good health (having been made ill with worry over your husband's excesses). You have no children which saddens you. You have some experience as a parson's wife in looking after poor children and the sick and the old.

You are a very kind person with a deep religious feeling. You were not very keen to come to the workhouse but having seen over it you realise there is a lot of work for you to do. You are very keen to help the children to avoid the problems of their pauper parents.

8.  You are an important member of the local church. You want to see plenty of religious education of the right sort given to the paupers. You hate all non-conformist Churchmen (Methodists and Baptists in particular). These 'sons of Satan' are a danger to the Church of England. You would oppose any Methodist candidate and point out how the Methodist Church has split from the Church of England. Who knows what revolution they are planning?

9.  You are the director of the workhouse in Poland Street. You are a hard and brutal woman. You run the workhouse for the unemployed and sick of the area. Anyone who can't get a job or who is too old or ill to work comes to the workhouse.

Like most Victorians, you think that people who are poor or unemployed are just *lazy*; good-for-nothings who ought to work hard like you do. You therefore make the workhouse as unpleasant a place as possible to encourage the poor to work harder to keep out of it.

*Conditions in the workhouse*

Families are split up as soon as they arrive. Women, men and children are kept separate and never meet. The men are employed smashing up rocks and the women pick ropes to pieces or sew mailbags. The food is kept to a basic minimum — plenty of thin carrot soup and suet. No meat of course, except on Sundays, when everyone gets half a sausage as a treat.

The poor are made to feel grateful for the help you give them. There are slogans painted on the walls — 'Be grateful for the generosity of the workhouse', 'God is good, God is kind' etc. Money for this charity comes from local rich people.

You see nothing wrong with this. You are saving people from starvation. If they want to leave all they have to do is get a job, but they're all too lazy to do that (actually you never allow them out to look for work). They are victims of their own laziness.

*Your importance to the inquiry — try to make the following points:*

a) You did not know Jack Straw personally, but knew him by reputation to be a typical, lazy good-for-nothing. He sometimes hung around the workhouse gate as if he were considering coming in. You have not seen him for a week.

b) Explain that there have been only 5 deaths in the workhouse from cholera, *but* these were all people who were brought to the workhouse hospital from Broad Street already suffering from cholera.

c) The workhouse has its own deep well and all water is drawn from this. No one is allowed out to get water from the pump.

d) Cholera comes from God. It is the revenge of God for the sins of the people. As the workhouse inmates have to spend three hours a day thanking God for all his mercies, they are well protected from it, while the sinful inhabitants of Broad Street are struck down in their hundreds — you can make much of this from the witness stand.

e) You know Dr Snow. He has been to the workhouse in the last week asking a lot of questions. He has a nosy character. You suspect him of being a 'do-gooder' who wants to question the way you run the workhouse. He kept asking questions about the well.

**10.** You are a rich factory owner. You would like to know if the new Master would be prepared to sell pauper children to work in factories for no wages. (Trade in these Pauper Apprentices is illegal.) You worked your way up from nothing so you don't see why the paupers should not as well.

11. You are the owner of Jackson's Mill. You are a typical Northern self-made man. You are the son of a Northampton shoemaker and went to work in a Manchester cotton factory at the age of 12. By your hard work you rose to the position of manager. In 1822, you bought a small disused warehouse and two new cotton-spinning machines and a loom on credit. By 1824, you had paid back the loans and bought new premises. From then on your business expanded rapidly and you have had a new factory built for you with 100 spinning machines and 20 steam-powered looms. You are one of the richest and most

respected mill owners in Manchester. You have a seat on the town council and a large mansion just outside the city with 20 rooms and 8 servants. You are married with 3 daughters.

You are a hard, tough man, having fought your way to the top. You consider yourself just as good as the idle rich who inherited their money. You worked hard for yours.

*Your importance to the inquiry — try to make the following points:*

a) You are amazed that your factory is being investigated. You consider yourself to be a model employer and wish to point out the following facts:

    i)   You are a kind and generous employer.

    ii)   You pay good wages — top rates. You provide houses with low rents for your workers.

    iii)   You have provided a factory shop where workers can buy goods with the tokens you give them for wages. (You have these token made in the workshop of Matthew Boulton and James Watt.)

    iv)   You have arranged for the town clock to strike 13 times at 1 p.m. so that the workers will not be late by missing the single bell and so lose wages.

    v)   You employ no children unless they can produce a certificate signed by a doctor saying their are probably over 13 and over 4' 3½" (128.75 cm) tall and so well able to stand the work.

b) You employ Henry Beech as factory overseer and manager. He is a good Christian and you see him in church every Sunday. He had excellent references and is firm but fair.

c) You are good friends with the factory inspectors who often come to your house. They have never criticised your factory.

*You may come under attack from the inquiry. You can always fall back on the following defence:*

a) You do not visit the factory a great deal nowadays (this is not quite true), so any questions about deformed children or low pay should be directed at Henry Beech. He more or less runs the factory by himself and you now concentrate on your civic duties.

b) You provide employment for the poor and needy — without factory owners like you they would have no jobs and would be starving.

c) As a child you worked for a lot less than the people earn in your factory and look how you have succeeded through hard work.

d) Anyone can rise to the top of the ladder by hard work. The opportunities are there for everyone and workers have only themselves to blame if their living conditions are bad. They should drink less and work harder.

e) Any attempt to limit the hours of work or increase the pay of workers would be a gross interference with the principles in which you believe, namely that the Government knows nothing about the running of factories and should leave business to the experts. Anyway, if restrictions were placed on factory owners, the price of goods would rise and the poor would be even worse off.

f) The prices in your shop may be a little higher than in other shops, but only because the goods are of superior quality. You can defend the use of metal tokens as your way of ensuring that the workers do not fritter away their wages on drink, which is not available in your shop.

**12.** You are a very important person — physician to Queen Victoria. You have been carrying out a survey of health conditions in the Broad Street area.

Over the last 10 days there has been the most terrible outbreak of cholera ever known in Britain, in Broad Street. Over 500 people have died.

*Your importance to the inquiry — try to make the following points:*

During your survey you have discovered the following things:

a) Housing conditions are bad, (overcrowding; damp, flooded cellars; no windows; rubbish and sewage in the streets), but no worse than anywhere else in London.

b) Most of the deaths have taken place near the Broad Street pump.

c) In the case of deaths which occurred nearer other pumps, the families of the deceased said they always went to the Broad Street pump as they preferred the taste of the water.

d) An examination of the Broad Street pump showed no signs of cholera germs.

e) None of the houses has its own water supply except the brewery and the workhouse in Poland Street (you interviewed the owner and director respectively). All the other inhabitants obtain their water from the Broad Street pump.

f) Facts about cholera:
   i) cholera breeds in polluted water;
   ii) cholera is contagious, spread by touch and polluted water;
   iii) the victim develops a heavy fever, becomes delirious, is unable to take solid food;
   iv) the cholera bacteria is difficult to pinpoint with present primitive techniques — crude microscopes etc.

g) You saw the body of Jack Straw briefly. You were unable to draw any conclusions except that he was uninjured. He was extremely thin. You believe it is likely he died of cholera.

h) The water is supplied by the Metropolitan water works. The pipes are mainly clay and have not been replaced for 30 years. The streets around the pump are thick with refuse and sewage.

i) You are very critical of Professor Craig's theory. Cholera is *not* caused by foul air from polluted rivers because:
   i) other towns with polluted rivers have not had cholera;
   ii) other areas in London close to the river have not had cholera;
   iii) *all* evidence points towards the Broad Street pump as the cause of cholera.

13. You are an important landowner. As a ratepayer you are worried that the cost of Poor Relief is rising. This is costing people like you more money. You would not like to see the new master being extravagant or giving the paupers much food.

14. You are a local doctor who has been appointed as surgeon to the prison. You have done this job for 3 years. You visit the prison about once every 2 weeks and are appalled by the conditions there. You are a person of good character and have an excellent reputation in the area. You have a number of important patients including Lord Hertston, the local landowner.
*Your importance to the inquiry — try to make the following points:*
a) Conditions in the prison are absolutely appalling. It is filthy, and sewage and rubbish lie around. Rats swarm around freely. There is no hospital (infirmary) and almost no

medicine. There are frequent outbreaks of jail fever (typhus). There have been 4 occurances of this while you have been surgeon. You are not surprised at this because of the filthy conditions there.

b) You have sent several written reports to the jailer and to the magistrate, Mr Allday, about the conditions but nothing has been done.

c) The prison is very badly run. Mr Allday has never been there perhaps because he feared he would catch typhus. The jailer and the turnkeys care nothing for the prisoners and do nothing to keep the place clean.

d) The prison is totally unsuitable because:

    i)   It is overcrowded.

    ii)   The building is old and in bad repair. The floors are earth and impossible to keep clean. The roof leaks. There is no proper drainage, and sewage just floats about on the floor.

    iii)   The cells are dark and airless. Many have no windows at all. Those that do are generally very small. The circulation of air throughout the prison is very bad.

    iv)   There are no proper beds. Prisoners have to sleep on damp straw on the floor.

    v)   Many prisoners are chained up all day long.

These problems make it impossible to keep the prison a healthy place. It smells so bad that you have all your clothes washed twice after each visit.

e) The prisoners are not fed enough. They have to buy most of their food from the jailer. Most cannot afford to have a proper diet.

*Your solutions:*

a) A new prison must be built. This should be properly ventilated and sound in construction. There should be no open sewers and the floors should be made of stone. It should be heated in winter.

b) A proper infirmary should be built. It must be fully equipped and well stocked with medicines.

c) Prisoners should be properly fed and not have to pay for their food.

d) The prison should be organised on the American 'Silent System'. This means that the prisoners are not allowed to talk to each other at all. Prisoners cannot have a bad influence on each other. To prevent them returning they should be made to fear prison. Prison life should be made as unpleasant as possible, but in a scientific way. Therefore you propose that 2 machines should be installed which would provide hard work but in a properly measured way. These machines are:

    i)   The **treadwheel**. On this prisoners walk on the spot turning a heavy wheel. They can be given scientifically measured amounts of walking.

    ii)   The **crank**. This is a device like a mangle where the prisoner turns a handle which lifts buckets of sand. The exact number of turns can be measured by a dial on the machine.

With these 2 devices prisoners could be made to earn their food and privileges by properly measured amounts of work.


**15.**   (Information in brackets to be kept secret as long as possible.)

Born in 1800. Your father was a soldier killed at Waterloo. You received a basic education in a local Church school (which you hated and as a result you no longer believe in God.)

Between 1816 and 1835 you worked in a cotton factory and worked your way up to become overseer by 1830. You married in 1835 and left your job. (You were in fact sacked for brutality to workers which resulted in the paralysis of one woman and the deaths of 2 children.) You were unable to find work in Manchester (because of your brutal reputation) so you moved south.

Since 1837 you have worked as a turnkey in Maidstone jail. (The prisoners hate and fear you for your brutal ways. You make a good income from them for supplying luxuries and not beating them up.) You are now looking for advancement. You are a strong candidate because of your wide experience in dealing with people.

You are respectable in appearance, if a bit on the rough side. You intend to carry on running the workhouse as it is at the moment with the following changes:

a)   You think there should be much firmer discipline. There have been riots in workhouses in Stockport and Bradford this year. There should be more flogging to show the inmates who is master. Children who wet the bed should be made to sleep in coffins in the dead house.

b)   You intend to cut the costs of running the workhouse by cutting down the meals. No meat would be allowed at all — it heats the blood and can cause violent behaviour. A hungry pauper is a quiet pauper.

Try to keep your violent temper under control throughout the interview!

**16.** (Information in brackets to be kept secret for as long as possible.)

Born in 1805. Your father was a carpenter. You had no education to speak of. Between 1817 and 1825 you worked in a public house serving drinks. (You have a slight drink problem as a result of this.)

In 1826 you were taken on as the landlady of a common lodging house in Maidstone. You were responsible for collecting rents and looking after the 65 girls who lived there. This gave you good practice in looking after the poor. (Many of the girls were earning money from illegal activities and you took money from them to keep quiet.)

You married in 1836. You have no children. You and your husband now live in a small house 2 miles from Maidstone Jail where he works. You do not work any more. Your husband has a difficult job as a turnkey. (He also has a violent temper and beats you up regularly. You are very afraid of him.)

**17.** You are a local doctor. You are very keen to make sure that the Master or Matron has some kind of medical training and that the workhouse hospital will be properly run.

**18.** You are a very low woman. You get work when you can cleaning, roadsweeping, shovelling the sewage out of the gutters etc. You are extremely poor and live in the common lodging house (see map on page 32) which is hopelessly overcrowded — 120 women live in 6 small rooms and sleep on heaps of straw on the floor. Many of the other girls work in match factories or sweatshops (small factories for making clothes) where they work long hours — 16 to 18 hours a day — for next to nothing. You are 28.

You knew Jack Straw very well and were hoping to marry him when he got a job. However, he had been unemployed for over two years — you don't know how he kept body and soul together. He slept rough in Broad Street in some disused houses which were full of rats and other vermin. He was 32.

74

You can make more of your role by telling stories of the horrors of London life.

*Your importance to the inquiry — try to make the following points:*

a) Living conditions in your street were no better than they were in Broad Street — *but* very few people have died from cholera in your area.

b) Jack Straw (though unfortunate and smelly) was a nice man — he did not have an enemy in the world. Nor did he have any money — so he was *not* murdered.

c) You had not seen him recently because he'd been ill (you don't know with what).

d) You didn't use the Broad Street pump and nor did your neighbours.

e) There have been *some* cholera deaths in your area — all of them school children who went to the Broad Street school. There have been *many* deaths from cholera in the Broad Street area. Jack might have been a victim.

Like everyone, you are terrified of the cholera epidemic. You have taken the normal precautions — drinking large amounts of salted water, smearing mustard on your feet, drinking plenty of gin and saying extra prayers. These obviously work well because you have not caught the disease.


**19.** You are the overseer of Jackson's Mill. You have had an interesting and varied career. You started life in the Navy. You were the Bosun's mate for 10 years and, as such, flogged over 1,000 men with the cat-o'-nine-tails (a whip) — quite normal procedure and vital for maintaining discipline. You left the Navy with nothing at the end of the Napoleonic Wars, in 1815, and drifted to Manchester. You got a job at Jackson's Mill, and your skill at handling people soon marked you out. You became foreman and lately overseer. You earn 8/- (40p) a week in cash.

You run the factory rather like a ship — plenty of clear rules and a thrashing for anyone who breaks them. All the rules are vital to the running of the factory — for example, if the windows are opened, the air will dry up and the cotton will break more easily; this will waste time and involve the workers in extra work knotting the yarn.

You have to keep to a strict schedule because Mr Jackson is a tough employer who visits the factory twice a day to check the books and inspect the machines. Anyone who is even a minute late loses two days' pay (1/- [5p] ).

You drink a modest amount — mainly rum, for which you developed a taste in your Navy days (in fact you drink about a bottle a day). You maintain a respectable front and go to church every Sunday.

*Your importance to the inquiry — try to make the following points.*

a) The workers are very lazy — the children are always falling asleep at their machines and hiding in the bales of cotton for a few minutes' sleep. You waste valuable time each week searching for them and livening them up with a few 'tickles' of your belt.

b) The workers are slow — many have chest complaints (probably from too much drinking) and stiff fingers (probably from a poor diet). The children fall asleep and get dragged into machines, ruining hundreds of yards of cloth which will be stained with blood. This is another good reason for keeping them awake.

c) You are giving employment to the poor. Mrs Jones, an old friend of yours, is the director of an orphanage in Portsmouth. She regularly sends orphans from there to the factory to learn a useful trade in the cotton industry.

d) You never employ children unless they have a doctor's certificate saying that they are probably over 13 years of age and over 4' 3½" (128.75 cm) tall and so well able to stand up to the work.

e) You are against the use of guards for the machines because they slow down their operation. They make it difficult for the children to climb into the machines to clean. (The machines aren't stopped, because this would cause delays and make the cloth more expensive.)

f) The factories are providing employment and wealth for the people of England. Government interference would stop them working efficiently. This would lead to wage cuts, so the workers would suffer the most.

g) The workers get very high wages, up to 3/- (15p) a week. They also get tokens (metal coins) which they can spend in Mr Jackson's well-stocked shop, where only the best goods are found at bargain prices. (You do not shop there yourself.)

h) You have never seen a factory inspector.

**20.** You are an important landowner. You are on the Boards of several institutions including the nearby jail. You know about the accepted practice that jailers and turnkeys accept money from prisoners to provide them with luxuries. You also know that many turnkeys are extremely brutal. You also want to know how the new Master and Matron would deal with violent or difficult paupers. Try them out by asking them what they would do with:

    a)   A child who wets the bed.

    b)   A pauper who returns from looking for work drunk.

    c)   A pauper who attacks a member of the workhouse staff.

    d)   A pauper who steals.

**21.** You are in prison for debt. You have to stay there until you have paid off the money you owe. You were sent to prison after your employer, a butcher, refused to pay you, then stole your savings and had you arrested saying you owed him £15.

Your wife is working hard as a servant to try to raise the money to have you released but you owe the jailer and the turnkeys over £12 which you have had to pay for food to keep alive. You despair of ever being released.

You think it is disgusting that an honest God-fearing person like yourself who is totally innocent has to mix with common criminals, the dregs of society. You have seen sights which would drive people mad.

*Your importance to the inquiry — try to make the following points:*

a) The prison building is extremely old and in appalling condition. The whole place is filthy with rubbish and sewage. The walls are running with water and covered in green slime. There are rats everywhere.

b) It is very overcrowded. There are 19 prisoners in your room which is about 3 metres square. There is no window. You all sleep on wet straw which is only changed once a month. Some of you have to sleep standing up. There is an open sewer running through the middle of your room. The smell is unbelievable. Almost everyone is ill. There was an outbreak of typhus (jail fever) last winter in which 32 people died.

c) You have to mix with the common criminals (felons) many of whom are very violent. There are many fights and much drunkenness. (Prisoners can buy drink at the prison taproom.) The prisoners behave like animals.

d) You are charged for everything. There is no food provided and you have to buy it from the turnkeys (warders). Turnkeys even charge for removing chains. The jailer can charge for food, furniture, firewood and any luxuries like tobacco that the prisoners want. Needless to say the prices are 4 or 5 times higher than they should be. The staff must make a huge profit. You understand that the jailer paid over £500 for his post.

e) You now owe the jailer and the turnkeys so much that you do not see how you can ever get out. On the very first day you arrived in the prison you had to buy all the prisoners in the jail a drink. If people refuse to pay this 'chummage' the other prisoners beat them, sometimes even kill them.

f) You think it is disgraceful that men, women and children are all mixed up together. This leads to much trouble and the children learn the bad ways of the adult criminals.

g) The turnkeys are brutes and seem as bad as the prisoners. They take delight in torturing the prisoners by chaining them, flogging them, beating them, throwing them into icy baths for hours on end and all manner of terrible treatments.

h) Prisoners who are sick receive little or no treatment. There is no hospital (infirmary) and the surgeon rarely visits.

*Your solutions:*

a) Crime is mainly caused by poverty and until the poor can be helped there will always be crime. The only solution is to cure poverty. People who fall into debt should not be locked away, but should be helped to pay off the money they owe.

b) People should be paid a decent wage and given proper living conditions. If they were, crime would disappear.

c) Prisoners should be trained to do a good job so that they do not turn back to crime when they are let out.

22. You are the director of an orphanage in Portsmouth, which is part of the parish workhouse. The children in the orphanage are the sons and daughters of poor people who have died or gone to prison. Their parents were often drunkards or criminals. You think of yourself as doing these children a great service by saving them from a life of poverty and crime.

*Conditions in the orphanage*

There is not much money to run the orphanage, so conditions there are rather basic. Children sleep in large dormitories on straw mattresses. Everything is clean, but there are no luxuries. Food is mainly porridge and soup; plenty of bread, but no meat. The orphans wear rough canvas clothes. All this is provided by charity.

The orphans receive some education in the 3Rs (reading, writing and arithmetic) but many of them are unable to read or write. The rules have to be pretty strict to maintain discipline and teach the children proper manners. There is little laughter and few pleasures. Any spare time is spent praying or thanking the Lord for his mercy in providing somewhere to live rather than the gutters or the rat-infested slums of the overcrowded towns.

*Your importance to the inquiry — try to make the following points:*

a)  You have known Mr Beech, the overseer of Jackson's Mill from his days in the Navy (and a frisky lad he was to). You now see him twice a year when he comes to the orphanage in a wagon to collect 15 boys and girls to take back to the factory to learn the trade of cotton spinning. You are very pleased to see these children so usefully employed in learning a trade.

b)  All the children are over the age of 14 as far as you know (although you have no way of checking this, since they have no birth certificates and they come to you at different ages).

c)  The children are all kept in good health by Mr Beech at the factory (he tells you this — you never see them again).

d)  Mr Beech is very kind to them calling them nicknames like 'matey', 'captain' and other nautical terms.

e)  He pays you a small amount for each child (about £2) which you spend buying meat for the poor orphans (actually you spend this on gin for yourself).

f)  Before 1822, Mr Beech used to take 30—40 children a year.

You can always hide behind a cloak of ignorance if the going gets rough — a good woman trying her best with too few resources.

23.  You are a nosy person who reads the papers and keeps up with all the latest gossip. You do not trust any of the candidates. Find out why Mr Rushbrook did not appear to be working between 1835 and 1837. Also, is Mr Bridge as good as he looks? Why does he want to leave his comfortable job to come to the

workhouse and why is he prepared to take a cut in salary?

24.   You are the owner of a textile factory. You are 47 and
married with 5 children. Your factory has made you very rich.
You live in a huge mansion 2 miles from the factory. You are
extremely upset by the loss of your factory. It will cost you
most of your fortune to rebuild it. You feel very bitter and
angry about this especially towards the magistrates and the
Government who have not acted firmly enough. You can be
very hostile and aggressive during the questioning.
   *Your importance to the inquiry — try to make the following
   points:*
   *Events leading to the attack.*
a)   A year ago you invested a lot of money in steam-powered
textile machinery. This helped you make cheaper cloth,
although unfortunately, you had to lay off about 160 (out of
250) workers.

b) Two weeks ago you received a threatening letter (part of
the written evidence, see page 10). You may explain what
this said *only* if you are asked directly. It has obviously been
written by an uneducated poor person because of the
spelling.

> 'We hear . . . that you [have] got shearing machines and
> if you don't pull them down in a fortnight's time we
> will pull them down for you. We will, you damned
> infernal dog. And before Almighty God we will burn
> down all the mills that have any shearing machines in
> [them]. We will cut out all your damned hearts as do
> keep them and we will make the rest eat them or else we
> will serve them the same.'
>                 Signed by King Ned Ludd.

c)   You were frightened by this. You have heard that the
followers of 'King' Ludd (called Luddites) have been
attacking   textile   factories   all   over   Nottinghamshire,
Lancashire and Yorkshire.

d) You informed the local magistrate and demanded that
your factory should be protected. He sent 50 soldiers but the
evening before the attack they were sent to a nearby town to
help put down a riot. You thought this was ridiculous as
there are over 5,000 soldiers in Yorkshire and 50 should have
been left with you.

e)   You hired 5 unemployed miners and with 4 of your

80

servants you barricaded the factory and defended it with muskets.

*The attack*

a) Last night a mob of over 200 men came to the factory. They carried muskets, pikes and large hammers. They had their faces blacked. They called on you to destroy your machines. You refused.

b) They attacked the factory. Shots were fired. 2 of your men were hurt — one has died. Several Luddites fell. The mob smashed down the doors with heavy hammers. You were struck on the head and lost consciousness.

c) When you awoke the factory was burning. You rode to the village for help. You awoke several of your workers but no one would help you. You were forced to stand by and watch your factory burn down to the ground. The Luddites had vanished. You did not recognise any of them.

*Why you think this happened*

a) Times are very bad for the workers. There have been a series of bad harvests and the poor are starving. There is much unemployment, especially among skilled workers made unemployed by machines.

b) The textile industry is in the middle of a depression. The reasons for this are:

   i)   The Government has started an ill-advised war against America which has cut off supplies of cotton to England.

   ii)  Napoleon has introduced his 'Continental System' where European countries are forbidden to buy British goods. This is strangling the textile industry.

   iii) The British Government has replied with 'Orders in Council' which have further reduced European trade. (The British Navy stops trade between French-controlled ports.)

As a result of all these measures factory owners have been forced to become more efficient to keep their prices down. This has meant that many more machines are used which in turn has thrown people out of work. This has caused starvation and trouble among the poor.

c) Many workers have joined together to protect their jobs. Luddites, followers of the legendary 'King' Ludd have begun to smash the machines which threaten their jobs. Recently they have become more violent and have burned down factories and even killed some factory owners.

*Your solutions:*

a) The Government should take stricter measures against Luddites. More soldiers should be used. Soldiers should live in villages.

b) Luddite leaders must be found and the death penalty should be brought in for machine-breaking. Luddites should be hanged.

c) The Government should stop interfering in trade. This is the main problem. The war with America should be stopped and somehow trade with Europe must be resumed. This will cause the textile industry to recover and there will be more jobs.

**25.** You are an important merchant. You are particularly concerned that paupers should be taught a useful trade. Will the Master keep up the present training scheme? On the other hand you do not want to see too much of the ratepayers' money being spent on extravagances.

**26.** You own the brewery in Broad Street. It is a very success-ful business. You send beer from your brewery by the new railways all over Britain. You think the railways are a marvellous invention — so quick and efficient.

You spend a good deal of your time tasting your beer (which you consider to be one of your most important jobs) and checking on its quality. This means, of course, that you spend most of your time drunk, or in an alcoholic haze, which accounts for your frequent losses of memory and fits of anger.

You are well aware of recent events in Broad Street and know that a lot of people have died from cholera in the last couple of weeks. You don't know exactly how many, but the funeral bells are always ringing and the carts clatter up and down the street carrying the bodies.

You know Dr Snow, a well-dressed busybody, who is always asking questions around Broad Street, and you suspect him of being a dangerous criminal trying to steal your secret beer recipe. You do not know Jack Straw, but vaguely remember a tramp who used to try to beg money from you. You sometimes kicked him out of your way.

*Your importance to the inquiry — try to make the following points:*

a)  Cast doubts on the character of Dr Snow. He kept asking questions about the amount of beer you drink, the amount of beer your workers drink and how you make the beer.

b)  Make the point that no one at your brewery has died of cholera.

c)  Everyone knows that cholera hits only heavy drinkers. Jack Straw was probably a heavy drinker and that was why he couldn't get a job.

d)  Explain that your employees are allowed to drink up to 10 pints of free beer a day with their meals, so they never bring water to work to drink. Many take beer home in bottles.

e)  There is a deep well at the brewery and water for brewing is obtained there.

27.  You are a young woman of 24 employed in Jackson's Mill. You have worked there for 4 years. Before that you worked as a coal heaver at a mine, loading coal on to barges. The work in the mill is not so hard, but it could be much better. Your fingers are twisted and deformed by the constant knotting of broken threads which is your job.

You live very close to the factory, about 200 yards away in a disgusting damp, little house owned by Mr Jackson. Your rent is deducted from your wages (the rent is 1/- [5p] per week).

Your husband is out of work because one of his legs was crushed in an accident at the iron foundry where he worked. You have 2 children — 2 boys, aged 8 and 6. They both work at the mill.

You all go to work at 6 a.m., and leave work at 8 p.m., but work longer hours if there is a rush on. You earn 3/- (15p) a week. The children, between them, earn 2/- (10p) per week; they do odd jobs and clean machines.

*Your importance to the inquiry — try to make the following points:*

a)  You have to send your children out to work in order to earn enough to live and to look after your sick husband.

b)  You have to do most of the housework as your husband cannot move around much and the children are too tired to help. By the time you have prepared the evening meal it is 10 or 10.30 p.m. If there is a rush on at the factory and overtime is required, it may be as late as 11.30 p.m. The children often cry while being fed and have to be shaken constantly to be kept awake.

c) The work is very hard — the younger boys walk or run 15 miles a day in the factory, fetching and carrying.

d) Mr Beech is a brute who beats any children who do not move fast enough or who fall asleep at their work.

e) The factory is very hot and damp — no windows can be opened for fear that the outside air may cause the cotton to snap. Many workers, including yourself, have chest complaints and often cough blood.

f) A large proportion of your wages is not paid in money, but in metal tokens which can be exchanged for food at the factory shop. The prices there are twice as high as in ordinary shops. The factory shop is owned by Mr Jackson.

g) There are many accidents in the factory, mainly caused by children falling into unguarded machines. They have to crawl around and under them while they are working.

h) Many of the workers are undernourished and overtired — this makes them slow to respond to orders and emergencies.

i) Although there are a few pauper apprentices, most children are the sons and daughters of workers at the factories. There are a number under the age of 9.

j) Normal hours of work: 6 a.m. to 8 p.m.
Hours of work during brisk time (a period of extra work): 3 a.m. to 9 p.m.
Normal pay for adults: 3/- per week (15p)
Wages during brisk time: 3/7½ (18p)
Wages for children: max. 2/- (10p) per week; usual 6d (2½p) per week
Pauper apprentices earn nothing.


28. You used to be in the Army. You have a vague recollection of someone called Bridge who was kicked out of the Army, but you cannot remember any details. Is this the same man?

As an ex-Army man you think the workhouse treats the paupers too well. They are all lazy scoundrels who should be flogged back to work. The new Master should be stronger on discipline.

**29.** You are uneducated and poor. You are a hardened criminal serving a 5-year sentence for robbery. You have been in prison 6 times before, mostly for theft. Your first experience of prison was when you were 10 and you learned a lot of useful tricks about picking locks and selling stolen property.

Because you are in prison for committing a crime and not for debt, you are known as a felon. In Hertston Prison, which is hopelessly overcrowded, debtors and felons are mixed together. There are also a number of female prisoners who are mixed in with the men — and some young children as well.

*Your importance to the inquiry — try to make the following points:*

a) Conditions in the prison are appalling. There are no proper facilities for washing. Rubbish is seldom collected. Prisoners are crowded into rooms. In your room there are 14 prisoners in a space 2½ metres square. An open sewer runs across the middle of the room and gives off a dreadful smell. The walls are running with water and covered in green slime. Prisoners sleep on damp straw on the floor. Many prisoners sleep standing up. There are rats everywhere.

b) The turnkeys are vicious and cruel. Many prisoners are chained up or wear shackles with heavy weights on. The turnkeys flog anyone who misbehaves or tries to protest. You know of 2 prisoners who died as a result of being beaten with chains.

c) The turnkeys charge for everything. All food, firewood, furniture, bedding and luxuries have to be paid for at very high prices (e.g. it cost 1/- (5p) to share a bed).

d) The food is dreadful, hardly fit for pigs. You are lucky to get fed every other day. The bread is stale and often mouldy. You soon use up the tiny amounts of money you get from working in the prison workshop. Any money brought by visitors has to be given to the turnkeys.

e) You do some work in the prison workshop. You make various things including rope and tools. The 'manufacturer' in charge, Mr Richards, is lazy and unfair. He underpays you and is often viciously drunk. You have managed to steal some rope and a file from the workshop.

f) You are allowed into the fresh air for exercise once a week for 10 minutes.

g) There is a general atmosphere of fear and despair in the prison. Most prisoners expect to die before they have served their sentences, probably from typhus (jail fever). The only hope is escape but even then you do not know how long you can stay out of trouble because you do not know any other life except crime.

h) Your only pleasure in the prison is the taproom (bar) where you can buy drink.

*Your solutions:*

a) You do not know what the answer is to the problem of prisons. Obviously they should not be pleasant places but surely criminals will never reform if they are treated like animals. They have no pride in themselves.

b) There should be some kind of rule book to stop the turn-keys beating the prisoners. Perhaps prisoners should be taught some useful trade so they can take up an honest life when they get out.

c) At present little attempt is made to reform prisoners apart from the visits of the chaplain who is an old idiot and can always be persuaded to hand over a few coppers if you pretend to be praying when he comes in or tell him that you have seen the error of your ways.

**30.** You are 31 and unmarried. You came to the area 5 months ago from Nottingham. You have worked in the textile industry all your life. You began as a 'stockinger' (making stockings) in Nottingham but were thrown out of work by the new stocking frames bought by the factory owners. These machines make the material much quicker than the old hand method but the stockings fall to pieces in a couple of weeks. This cheap, shoddy material has knocked the bottom out of the market and thrown hundreds of skilled workers into unemployment. This had led to riots and machine-breaking.

Desperate for work, you went to the local magistrate and landlord, Squire Stockby, and volunteered to become a spy on the machine-breakers. You have worked your way up their ranks and have now risen quite high. You may reveal any or all of the following things about the Luddites.

*Luddites*

a) Luddites are followers of Ned Ludd. No one has ever seen him and most people do not think he really exists.

b) The headquarters of the Luddites is in Sherwood Forest.

c) Luddites are unemployed textile workers dedicated to destroying the machines that have put them out of work.

d) Every member of the Luddites takes a secret oath (which is against the law) never to give away the secrets of the group.

e) Luddites recognise each other by secret signs. (One raises the right hand over the right eye — the other replies by raising the left hand over the left eye. The first touches the right corner of the mouth with the right forefinger — the other replies with the left forefinger to the left corner of the mouth. The first asks 'What are you?'; reply — 'Determined'; then 'What for?'; reply — 'Free Liberty.')

f) There are thousands of members — many of them skilled workmen.

g) The members meet in small groups to talk. They collect money to buy arms (1d (½p) a week from each member).

h) They train with weapons such as muskets, pikes, pistols and clubs. They have very good discipline, rather like an army.

i) The heroes of the Luddites are the people who carry large hammers called 'Enochs' to smash machines.

j) With their knowledge of the local area, the Luddites can easily avoid the clumsy, noisy soldiers.

k) No one will give the Luddites away because they threaten traitors with death, and anyway, most workers who are starving and unemployed approve of the Luddites.

l) Luddites are everywhere in Nottingham, Yorkshire and Lancashire. They are too well-organised to be just ignorant workers. You suspect that they may be led by some important, educated people. These could be noblemen who are fed-up with the King; or supporters of the French; or Catholic traitors. You are not quite sure.

*Payments*

(You are fairly reluctant to reveal the exact amounts.)

Squire Stockby and his rich friends pay you the following bounties:

£50 for each Luddite leader identified

£100 for each riot revealed

£1000 for conclusive evidence that the Luddites intend to overthrow the Government and start a revolution.

As a result of your information 9 Luddite leaders have been arrested. You have helped to organise a number of raids on factories and then told the authorities. This has earned you quite a lot of money. You are sure that if you are given enough time you will be able to uncover a revolution. You are pretty certain it is a revolutionary movement and you have told Squire Stockby this many times. You were not able to reveal the attack on Swan's factory because you were ill (drunk).

*Your solutions:*

a) You should be given more time and a lot more money to discover the identities of the leaders and the extent of the plot.

b) You have to move cautiously and slowly because you could be betrayed or make some fatal mistake. The Luddites would not hesitate to kill a traitor. Even now you are trying to persuade them to become more violent so they can be caught in the act of committing a serious crime such as murder or treason.

**31.** You are in charge of the whole prison. You have to see that the other staff do their duties, keep the building in good repair and make sure that the prisoners see the error of their ways.

You have been doing the job for 15 years. You live about a mile away from the prison and go there regularly once a week. You leave the everyday running of the prison to your turnkeys (warders) who are all hand-picked for their toughness.

During your time as jailer you have not been paid a penny but have to make whatever you can from the prisoners. You feel you do a reasonable job considering all the difficulties and you resent this inquiry. These people are just interfering do-gooders. How many of them have ever been inside a prison or know the problems of dealing with violent criminals?

*Your importance to the inquiry — try to make the following points:*

a) The building is really totally unsuitable. It was built as the town jail in 1417 to hold 35 prisoners. It now holds 206. The county authorities have spent very little money on repairs or improvements. Mr Allday never visited the prison.

b) You receive very little money from the county to supply food for the prisoners. What you do receive is based on an Act of 1572 when the price of bread was half today's price. There is no money provided for bread for debtors. There is nothing left over to improve the prison.

c) In order to make ends meet you have to take the perfectly legal steps of charging the prisoners. This money is called 'Fees'. You are allowed to charge fees for food, firewood, furniture, bedding and luxuries. You also make money by selling drink in the prison taproom and your licence to do this was granted by Mr Allday. You draw your own pay and that of your turnkeys from these fees.

d) There are few individual cells which means that you are forced to mix young and old; men and women; and innocent and guilty together. This is not a good state of affairs but it is forced on you by the unsuitability of the building.

e) The outside walls, the locks and the bars are in a poor state of repair which means that you are forced to chain up many of the prisoners all the time. Remember that many of them are very violent so this is a sensible precaution. You are satisfied that your turnkeys are never unnecessarily cruel.

f) By and large you allow the turnkeys to get on with their job. It is very difficult to control over 200 prisoners (many of whom are little better than animals) with only 6 men. It is hard to get anyone willing to do the work — so better not to ask too many questions.

*Your solutions:*

a) At present there are just too many prisoners. There are over 200 crimes for which people can be hanged but far too many people are being let off by soft-hearted juries. The answer is to hang more of them and not send them to unsuitable prisons for long sentences.

b) Failing this, if criminals are not hanged then they should be sent to some faraway country and not allowed to return (this is known as 'transportation'). They could work as slaves on the sugar plantations in the West Indies. Special prison colonies could be set up in one of the newly discovered countries like Australia. This could get rid of the problems of crime forever.

c) Whatever happens there must be no soft treatment of criminals. They just take advantage of any kindness shown to them. They must be punished. Punishment is the only cure for the criminal.

32.   You are very concerned that the reputation of Westford Workhouse as a place where the Poor Law is properly run, should be kept. You think that the very small number of punishments given to paupers (16 in 1840; 29 in 1841) is complete proof of the success of the present methods. You would not support anyone who would bring more cruel treat-

ment to the workhouse. This would only cause more problems and make the paupers more violent.

**33.** You are a professor of medicine at Glasgow University. You have made a special study of epidemic diseases, especially cholera. You are the leading world specialist on epidemics.

You have done some research into the Broad Street cholera epidemic. You have examined many bodies including Jack Straw's. You are certain he died of cholera.

*Your importance to the inquiry — try to make the following points:*

a) Facts about cholera:
    i)   cholera is infectious — it spreads through the air;
    ii)  cholera victims have painful cramps, a high fever and are unable to take solid food.

b) You examined the water from all the pumps in the Broad Street area. None of them contained cholera germs (including the Broad Street pump). This is yet another piece of evidence which destroys the arguments of those who claim that cholera is a water-borne disease.

c) Broad Street is typical of areas where cholera is found:
    i)   It is near a river — there are mudbanks and swamps nearby.
    ii)  It is on low-lying land with poor drainage.
    iii) The whole area and all the houses are damp.
Cholera is always found in low-lying industrial towns near rivers.

d) The cholera breeds in the swampy areas and is blown by the wind into places like Broad Street. People breathe the damp, infected air, then catch cholera and die.

e) The answer to cholera is to drain the swamps and dredge the rivers so they flow faster. In this way the cholera germs cannot breed.

f) Dr Snow is a dangerous quack who knows nothing of science or scientific method. His theories are absurd and not based on any proper evidence.

**34.** Born in 1810. Your father was a wealthy sea captain and a deeply religious man who devoted much of his life to helping the poor. You were brought up in a religious atmosphere. You received a good basic education from your father.

In 1828 you were converted to Methodism. You believe

strongly in the Methodist virtues of being sober, thrifty and hard-working. In 1828 you helped to start a charity school in the East End of London. Here you teach very poor children the basics of reading and writing. There is a great deal of Bible study and scripture.

You do not believe in the rules of the Church of England and you would run all the services yourself, including taking Holy Communion, although you are not a minister.

You do not believe in violence and punishment. You would try to run the workhouse on the teachings of the Bible and lots of love and attention. You would try to raise as much money as possible from local sources to try to improve the life of the paupers, giving them better food and a better education.

**35.** Born in 1815. Your father was a Methodist minister. You are very religious and believe strongly in the Methodist virtues of being thrifty, sober and hard-working. You met your husband in 1832 and married in 1833. You have helped him in the running of his charity school in the East End of London.

You are not very strong or well. You sometimes have unexplained fits when you shiver and are unable to speak. These do not last very long. During them you feel very close to God.

You have a very wide experience of working with poor people. You help to run many charitable institutions including a soup kitchen where you provide basic meals for the starving. You also visit prisoners in jails in London to try to bring them comfort. You have organised religious services in jails.

**36.** You are very interested in keeping the workhouse a respectable place. You would oppose any candidate who did not have a respectable background. You would be deeply suspicious of anyone with odd religious habits.

# Further Hints and Advice to the Teacher

## Preliminary Work

a) Choose your witnesses carefully. Good witnesses will enhance the roleplay enormously. Witnesses should be called in the order indicated in each introduction. You could have a practice session with them.

b) Suggestions for props and extras are included in 'Notes on individual roleplays' (see page 94). Elaborate preparations are not essential.

c) The roleplays are best used as introductions to topics. They will stimulate pupils to do the necessary follow-up work, notes etc. Do not teach all the facts and information in advance or the impact of the witnesses will be lost. Give a minimum introduction and background with, perhaps, 3 or 4 slides.

d) Classes can be prepared for the inquiry with your help by compiling lists or tables of questions to be asked. These can be drawn up for homework. They can easily be filled in during the inquiry. Extra questions can be added as the inquiry proceeds. There are some ideas for this in the exercises themselves.

A short example appears opposite which might be used for Jackson's Mill.

e) Teachers can take a role. It is often best to pick a crucial one and appear near the end. You can then slip in important ideas missed in earlier questions. If you prefer you can take a more neutral chairperson's role or devise a character of your own.

f) The last roleplay on Westford Workhouse should give you a good idea of other roles and extras you can add yourself to the other 4 should you so choose.

g) There is no reason why women cannot play men's roles and vice versa. On the other hand you will find the roles are fairly neutral and with a minimum of change will be suitable for the witness's spouse, i.e. Mr Taggart could appear instead of Mary, etc.

| Personal details | Reliability |
|---|---|
| Name . . . . . . . . . . . . . . . . . . . . . . . Occupation . . . . . . . . . . . . . . . . . | |
| Age. . . . . . . . . . . . . . . . . . . . . . . Marital Status . . . . . . . . . . . . . . . Pay . . . . . . . . . . . . . . . . . . . . . . . etc. | Reasons |

| Information |
|---|
| a) Hours of work |
| b) Pay |
| c) Conditions |
| d) Pauper apprentices |
| e) Dangers |
| etc. |

# Running the roleplay

You will find that pupils become more adept at asking questions as they have more practice. However, be prepared to ask important questions yourself and do not hesitate to start discussions with the class wherever you feel it is appropriate. You can draw the threads together at any time, suggest fruitful lines of enquiry, question the reliability of witnesses etc. Refer to the relevant roles to help you.

# Follow-up work

a) Use the follow-up exercises exactly as you yourself want. They overlap to some extent and it is not envisaged that all pupils will do all the exercises. Most pupils will be able to do about 6 out of 12. (Note — the Luddite roleplay has only 8 and the Workhouse has considerably more.) Lower ability pupils would do nos. 1 to 6; middle ability pupils, 3 to 9; and upper ability 6 to 12. This will vary according to the group and your own inclinations.

Much of the work is suitable for oral or group work. It does not have to be written. Early exercises tend to concentrate on the inquiry and later ones seek to widen the investigation.

b) Where reports are to be written, pupils find it very helpful if each section of the report is broken down into smaller sub-headings by the teacher. This will also stop them missing out essential points from their written work. These sub-headings will often be closely related to their question tables and the exercises. You should decide in advance the extent of the information you wish them to extract.

# Notes on individual roleplays

### 1. Mr Swan's Factory

This is a fairly simple roleplay. Hopkins' evidence is especially crucial. He can be played as a suspicious, elusive character or a secretive, frightened one. Bare feet for Sarah and a shawl will add character. Swan should look very respectable with dark topcoat and cravat. Hopkins should look richer than the unemployed worker he is. An extra character could be a magistrate giving evidence of Luddites he has convicted, to reveal the wide extent of the problem.

There are fewer follow-up exercises to give teachers the chance to discuss the whole question of witness reliability, bias etc. The implications of biased evidence will be important in later inquiries.

### 2. Jackson's Mill

Bare feet and a shawl etc. for Mary. Albert should look very ragged and can be played very well by a good 1st or 2nd year pupil imported from another class. A handkerchief stained with red ink or paint can be produced by Mary when she coughs so it seems as if blood has appeared on it. Beech should wear a heavy leather belt which he taps significantly and swig from a 'bottle of rum'. Emily should be neat but blousy. A suitable hat and shawl will help. She can sip discreetly from a small bottle of 'chest medicine'. Jackson should appear last and be a heavy and respectable character — a Northern self-made man. An interesting extra character is the shopkeeper. Some creative writing can be done on James Denman.

### 3.  Hertston Prison

Prisoners should look dirty and ill. Prisoner 1 should protest innocence at every opportunity.

Surgeon and chaplain should dress respectably and may not like each other. The jailer is a good teacher role.


### 4.  Broad Street

Emily is very poor — shawl and bare feet. Huggins can display signs of a drink problem and is fairly flashy. Mrs Pinch is severe and sombre with strong moral and religious overtones. Snow and Craig are both eminent people and should wear dark top-coats. A brief explanation of workhouses could be useful.

Pupils will gravitate towards a murder theory. To offset this, teachers can make up a small table based on exercises 1 and 2 so that pupils can cross off unlikely causes of death as the first witness, Emily, is interviewed. This should lead them towards cholera being the cause of death early on which makes later questions easier. The cause of death can be discussed before the next witness is called. Cholera, incidentally, is only the most likely cause — the evidence being largely circumstantial — and some pupils may still opt for a more open verdict. Everyone should do exercise 4.


### 5.  Westford Workhouse

This is more detailed than the other roleplays and it is suggested that it is not attempted until pupils have tried at least one of the others. It may suggest elaborations for earlier inquiries.

Each pupil should have a role. (They can share the 12 that have been written, or you can write some more, in accordance with the numbers in your class.) The pupils taking these 12 roles should copy out their roles and not refer to the back of the book again, to reduce 'snooping' on the roles of the main characters. A strict time limit should be placed on them while they do this.

Pupils are divided into mixed ability groups to complete one set of exercises per group (from numbers 1—5) as in the instructions *before* witnesses are interviewed. Exercise 4 — **Rules**, is the most difficult set of exercises; Exercise 1 — **Paupers**, involves some simple maths. Teachers can add their own lessons, slides, tapes etc. to this section to present as full a picture of workhouses as possible.

In the discussion on the workhouse pupils should be encouraged to speak in their characters if they can. The information given points to a well-run workhouse which is unpleasant but not vicious. The discussion may harden attitudes.

If 3 couples are not available, one person from each couple can represent the views of both by referring to the spouse's role.

Lower ability pupils will find the follow-up exercises 8—12 very difficult, so they can do some work from 1—5 which they have not done. The word puzzle could be done as a class activity. Exercise 7 could replace written reports.

An appointment must be made. The posts cannot be re-advertised. After the appointment has been made, the teacher can discuss each of the candidates, revealing in full any secret information which did not emerge.